Divergence of risk indicators and the conditions for market discipline in banking

GW00601999

Divergence of Risk Indicators and the Conditions for Market Discipline in Banking

by
Jens Forssbæck

SUERF – The European Money and Finance Forum
Vienna 2011

SUERF Study 2011/4

CIP

Divergence of risk indicators and the conditions for market discipline in banking

Authors: Jens Forssbæck

Keywords: bank risk; risk indicators; subordinated debt; market discipline; panel data

JEL Codes: G10; G21; G28

Vienna: SUERF (SUERF Studies: 2011/4) – November 2011

ISBN: 978-3-902109-59-0

© 2011 SUERF, Vienna

TABLE OF CONTENTS

Divergence of risk indicators and the conditions for market discipline in banking

Jens Forssbæck

Abstract

Accurate measurement of bank risk is a matter of considerable importance for bank regulation and supervision. Current practices in most countries emphasize reliance on financial statement data for assessing banks' risk. However, the possibility of increased reliance on market-based risk indicators has been a topic for academic and regulatory debate for a long time. Market monitoring of bank risk has typically been tested by regressing market-based risk indicators on various benchmark indicators (such as accounting ratios and credit ratings) to detect whether the market tracks bank risk. This approach overlooks the methodological 'unobservability' problem that testing one imperfect proxy indicator against another, when the true value (in this case, a bank's 'true' risk) is unknown, must yield limited conclusions as to the appropriateness of either indicator – particularly in the event of failure to establish a significant association. This paper assesses the relative information content of different risk indicators indirectly by associating the divergence between these indicators with the institutional setting. Empirical results for a large panel of banks worldwide suggest that market-based indicators are often more accurate than accounting indicators for high levels of institutional quality. In particular, spreads on subordinated debt may be more informative than either equity-based or accounting-based measures if the institutional conditions for market discipline to function are favourable. In addition, a combination measure incorporating both accounting and market data has superior accuracy regardless of the level of institutional quality, indicating that market data may contain complementary information on risk. These results cast doubt on the validity of the conclusions drawn in several previous studies that reject market discipline based on the finding that market-based risk indicators do not correspond well with various standard non-market indicators.

1. Introduction

Accurate measurement of banks' risk is important for several reasons. Regulators need to keep track of banks' risk behaviour because of the particular incentive structure facing banks (especially bank shareholders) due to their financing pattern, which is in large part insured debt, and because of the potential systemic consequences of excessive risk taking in banks. In addition, many recent proposals for improvement of bank regulation depend on accurate measurement of banks' risk (such as risk-based capital adequacy requirements, risk-based deposit insurance premia, etc.). Current practices among regulators in most countries emphasize reliance on financial statement data for the measurement of banks' risk (see, e.g., European Commission, 2008). However, the possibility of increased reliance on market discipline as a regulatory mechanism is a long-standing issue of study and debate for academics and regulators (see, e.g., Calomiris, 1999).

Market discipline (in banking) is commonly defined as a combination of *monitoring* and *influence* (see, e.g., Flannery, 2001; Bliss and Flannery, 2002), where 'monitoring' refers to the process whereby market participants (holders of various classes of bank capital) collect information on the bank's financial condition and market prices on bank claims reflect this information, and 'influence' refers to the market's capacity to actually get the bank to adjust its risk behaviour in accordance with the signals generated by fluctuations in market prices.

Primarily, research interest has circled around the former aspect of market discipline: can market prices on banks' outstanding securities be relied upon to convey accurate and useful information about banks' risk? The vast majority of papers testing the risk sensitivity of market prices perform (linear) regressions of some market-based measure of bank risk (e.g. the spreads on the bank's subordinated debt) on a set of other risk measures – typically accounting information and/or ratings. The establishment of a significant relationship between the market-based measure and the benchmark measure(s) is interpreted as a sign that the market adequately prices risk, and thus that market discipline would be a useful mechanism to restrain excessive risk taking by banks. Equally importantly, failure to establish a significant relationship is interpreted as absence of market discipline.

There are several methodological problems with this general approach (including, for instance, various specification problems related to functional form, omitted variables, etc. – see, e.g., Gorton and Santomero, 1990, and Pennacchi, 2001). In this paper, I focus on the fact that this general approach (and thus much of the empirical literature in this field) overlooks an *unobservability problem*, which limits the scope for interpreting the results in terms of the prospects for market discipline in general. The problem essentially lies in benchmarking one imperfect proxy (based on market prices) on other imperfect proxies (based on accounting information, ratings, etc.) of an unknown fundamental variable, *viz.* 'true' risk. It is not possible to know a priori which proxy contains the more accurate information on risk, and therefore – in the event of failure to establish a statistically significant association between the left-hand side variable and the right-hand side variable(s) – it is not possible to infer which side of the equation is 'wrong'. Using accounting information, ratings, and other commonly used risk proxies as benchmarks effectively entails restricting the definition of 'success' to correspondence with another, already available and imperfect measure. The implication is that (i) market prices can never contain more (useful) information than the benchmark measures (and whenever market prices do not correspond with the benchmark measures they are irrelevant), and (ii) therefore, indirect market discipline as a supervisory tool is superfluous, because all the information we need or could possibly hope to extract is already incorporated in already available measures. In a manner of speaking, market information is then not 'allowed' to contain any more information than we already have.

The purpose of this paper is to devise and implement a simple methodology which addresses this unobservability problem, and by which it is possible to identify if, which, and under what circumstances, market-based measures may contain more information than certain common benchmark measures. This is an important question for assessing the potential merits of market discipline, because although it may be relatively uncontroversial to suggest that market-based risk indicators contain *complementary* information, one of the points with market discipline is that the indicators are observed continuously (whereas, e.g., financial statement data are only observed at an annual or quarterly basis). It is therefore of interest to assess the informativeness of market-based indicators *individually*.

The paper uses an unobserved-variables approach to associate the divergence between different risk indicators on the one hand, with proxies of the conditions for market discipline to function on the other (these conditions are mainly various indicators of institutional quality), and identifies implied functional relationships of differences in relative information content in the included risk measures. The approach is essentially a systematization of the simple idea that if the disconnection between a market-based risk indicator and some benchmark indicator is greater when the conditions for market discipline are well satisfied (that is, when market-based risk measures *should* be relatively accurate), then it may be the benchmark indicator, rather than the market-based indicator, that is relatively less informative.

The methodology is implemented empirically on a panel of several hundred banks worldwide between the years 1994 and 2005. The results suggest that market-based risk measures are less informative than accounting indicators of risk for most levels of institutional quality, but that market-based indicators are often *more* informative if the conditions for market discipline to work are well satisfied (if the institutional quality is high). Specifically, spreads on subordinated debt are more informative than accounting-based risk indicators for the highest level of institutional quality. On the other hand, stock return volatility proves to be less informative than the accounting indicators for all observed levels of institutional quality. A combination measure incorporating both accounting and market data, finally, has superior accuracy regardless of the level of institutional quality, indicating that market data always contains complementary information on risk.

The paper is structured in the following way. Section 2 contains a selective review of literature addressing the conditions for market discipline and a brief run-down of empirical literature testing market monitoring in banking. Section 3 describes the methodology and develops the hypotheses, whereas Section 4 presents the estimation methods and the data. In Section 5, the empirical results are reported, and Section 6, finally, concludes.

2. MARKET DISCIPLINE AND BANK RISK – CONCEPTS, RESULTS, AND METHODOLOGICAL PROBLEMS

2.1. Market discipline

In principle, any holder of a risky claim on the bank which is tradable on a market could instil market discipline on banks. Holders and prospective buyers of the claim would have an incentive to monitor the bank's risk taking, and would therefore discipline banks' risk-taking directly, by (incrementally) influencing the bank's cost of capital, and indirectly, by providing a signal (in the form of the market price of the claim) to the bank itself, to the supervisory authority, and to other stakeholders, of the market's assessment of the bank's risk behaviour. Indirect market discipline could be imposed, e.g., by using such price signals as triggers for prompt corrective action (PCA) or for on-site examinations by the supervisory authority, or as basis for setting risk-adjusted deposit insurance premia.

The indirect and direct dimensions of market discipline are captured by the widely used definition of market discipline as a combination of *monitoring* and *influence* (see, e.g., Flannery, 2001; Bliss and Flannery, 2002). Monitoring captures the information aspect of market discipline: current and prospective claimants on the bank inform themselves of the bank's condition and set prices on their claims accordingly. Influence refers to the mechanism by which banks, in order to avoid the adverse consequences of stronger discipline (such as higher financing costs and closer monitoring by market participants as well as regulators) decrease their risk exposure (or, indeed, avoid increasing it in the first place).

The literature on market discipline in banking is mostly empirical (see next subsection), but more or less implicit in the empirical applications are assumptions on a couple of underlying questions, which have received some – but rather limited – treatment elsewhere. The first relates to the *conditions under which market discipline can be expected to 'work'* – i.e., a systematization of the basic requirements on the institutional setting that need to be satisfied for the market to (be able to) fulfil its task as disciplinarian. The second concerns *whether market prices of some classes of claims on banks are better able to produce useful signals of bank risk*. This second question is related to the first one insofar as its answer may depend on differences in the extent to which the conditions for market discipline are satisfied for different classes of claims on the bank.

As a general treatment of the first question, Lane (1993) sets up four conditions for market discipline to work[1]: (i) open capital markets; (ii) good information about a borrower's existing liabilities[2]; (iii) no prospect of a bailout (the supplier of financing must not benefit from third-party guarantees issued on the claim); and (iv) responsiveness of the borrower to market signals. Of these four conditions for market discipline in general, the first three concern primarily the monitoring aspect, whereas the fourth directly reflects the influence aspect. The monitoring aspect of market discipline is equivalent to the requirement that market signals accurately reflect risk; if they do, then the conditions for market monitoring of risk are satisfied. Therefore, market monitoring (the extent to which risk information is impounded in market prices) is conditioned on the openness of capital markets, the quality of the available information about the issuer of the security, and whether or not there are guarantees or insurance attached to the claim. However, if monitoring is costly, it is unlikely that market participants will expend costs for monitoring banks that are unresponsive to market signals (Llewellyn, 2005); thus, the monitoring aspect of market discipline is somewhat conditional on the influence aspect, so that the expectation of finding risk-relevant information in market prices becomes conditional on all four conditions. I will rely on this general grouping of market-discipline conditions in the empirical part of the paper.

The answer to the question if some types of claimants are more apt to exert market discipline than others is more ambiguous. One class of debtholders usually precluded from the discussion altogether, however, are (small) deposit holders. They are generally considered more or less immune to bank risk, since under deposit insurance, they have little incentive to monitor bank risk and instil market discipline. On the other hand, it is often considered that holders of *risky* debt (such as unsecured, or subordinated, bonds and notes) would act as better monitors of bank risk than equity holders (see, for instance, Calomiris, 1999; Evanoff and Wall, 2000; Sironi, 2001; Benink and Wihlborg, 2002). The argument largely rests on the notion that the risk-shifting incentives of shareholders resulting from the option value of equity in the presence of deposit insurance (Merton, 1977) make shareholders too inclined toward risk to serve as effective disciplinarians. Conversely, the focus of bondholders on downside risk means that their incentives are more or less in line with those of the supervisor/deposit insurer, and consequently that prices of uninsured debt would better reflect default risk (or at least be a more relevant risk meter for supervisors) than equity prices.

---

[1] Lane presumes a debt claim, but these conditions for market discipline should hold more generally for any type of risky claim.

[2] Presumably, one would add to this information about the borrower's assets and/or income streams.

It is not clear if this argument stands up to closer inspection. The relatively scant theoretical research that exists (Levonian, 2001; Nivorozhkin, 2005) suggests that spreads on subordinated debt would more accurately reflect default risk than equity prices only under certain conditions (associated with, *inter alia*, the relative shares of insured and uninsured debt, and the magnitude of bankruptcy costs). Some criticism voiced against the idea of relying on debt market discipline rests on the more mundane and practical point that stock markets are typically much more liquid than debt markets, and that bond spreads would be noisy signals of risk because the risk information is obfuscated by large liquidity premia (see, e.g., Saunders, 2001). The question whether stock prices or bond spreads better reflect bank risk is therefore to some extent an empirical one.

I next turn to a brief run-down of some main empirical results, and then turn to the particular methodological problem that is the focus of interest in this paper.

2.2. Evidence on market monitoring of bank risk

Tests of monitoring by holders of risky bank claims have typically been conducted by one of two main approaches. The first general method – which I will hence-forth refer to as the 'risk-sensitivity approach' – consists in regressing some market-based risk indicator on a set of benchmark risk measures (typically credit ratings and/or various accounting ratios) and control variables. If the benchmark risk measures are found to be significant determinants of the market signal, the result is taken as evidence of market self-regulation of bank risk; conversely, absence of significant associations between the market and the benchmark indicator(s) is interpreted as a rejection of market monitoring.

In the other main approach – which may be termed the 'early-warning approach' – market-based risk measures are tested as *predictors*, or leading indicators of actual bank failure, of insolvency, or of general deterioration of financial status (defined in different ways). Both these general approaches have been applied to both equity- and debt-based risk indicators with varying results. In what follows, I will focus on the risk-sensitivity approach.

A number of early studies test the sensitivity of the interest cost of large (and hence uninsured) certificates of deposit (CDs) or of the spreads on subordinated notes and debentures (SNDs) issued by US banks during the 1980s to various accounting measures of risk, using straightforward linear regression specifications. The results of these studies are, taken together, fairly inconclusive: whereas, for instance, Avery *et al.* (1988) and James (1990) find little evidence of accounting risk reflected in debt prices, other studies find that CD rates or SND spreads are significantly determined by at least some balance sheet items (Hannan and Hanweck, 1988; James, 1988; Keeley, 1990). Pointing out that theory predicts a non-linear relation between risk premia on debt and balance-sheet measures of risk, Gorton and Santomero (1990) derive implied asset volatilities from sub-debt spreads, and regress them on accounting indicators (using the same dataset as Avery *et al.*, 1988), but do not find evidence in support of the market-monitoring hypothesis. Brewer and Mondschean (1994), on the other hand, find evidence that the quality of banks' assets is reflected in both CD rates and in stock return volatilities.

Several later studies report relatively consistent evidence in support of market monitoring by sub-debt holders, using credit ratings, or ratings changes, as benchmark risk measures (Jagtiani *et al.*, 2002; Sironi, 2002, 2003; Pop, 2006). Hall *et al.* (2001) and Krishnan *et al.* (2006), on the other hand, are unable to produce evidence of ratings being reflected in various equity-based risk measures or in bond spreads, respectively. Event studies on announcement effects of ratings changes further complicate the picture: Berger and Davies (1998) find no announcement effects on abnormal stock returns, whereas Gropp and Richards (2001) find significant effects on stock returns but not on bond returns.

Considerations regarding the underlying conditions for market discipline often explicitly or implicitly factor into the research design of a large part of this literature (as previously noted). The 'no-bailout' condition, for example, is addressed by a number of papers. Thus, the conjectural government guarantees possibly associated with banks being 'too big to fail' are considered by Ellis and Flannery (1992) and Morgan and Stiroh (2001). Both papers find evidence of a 'too-big-to-fail' effect. Accounting for possible differences in the extent of implicitly issued guarantees under different regulatory regimes, Flannery and Sorescu (1996) and Hall *et al.* (2004) reach different results: whereas Flannery and Sorescu find that a more credible commitment to a no-bailout policy on the part of the deposit insurer leads to higher sensitivity of sub-debt yield spreads to underlying credit risk, Hall *et al.* find no such effect. The condition that markets must have good information about the borrower is also addressed by Morgan and Stiroh (2001). Their findings indicate that the market is tougher on more opaque banks, in terms of the sensitivity of sub-debt spreads to variations in asset quality.

A number of studies address various methodological problems associated with the standard risk-sensitivity approach to testing market monitoring[3]. At the focus

---

[3]   The issue of non-linearity between bond spreads and standard accounting-based risk indicators, as addressed by Gorton and Santomero (1990), has already been mentioned. This and other potential specification errors inherent in the standard risk-sensitivity approach, including possible omitted-variables problems, are addressed by Flannery and Sorescu (1996) and Pennacchi (2001). Other contributions, for instance Covitz *et al.* (2004) and Goyal (2005), argue that the association between spreads on risky debt and standard benchmark risk measures may be underestimated unless it is taken into account that riskier banks may avoid issuing sub-debt in the first place (in order to avoid being disciplined), or that they may be forced to accept a higher number of restrictive covenants being included in the debt contracts. Covitz *et al.* (2004) find limited evidence in support of the former hypothesis, whereas Goyal (2005) finds that risk significantly determines covenants included in sub-debt issues.

of interest for the remainder of this paper is the *unobservability problem* described in the introduction[4]. The problem is this: If the existing benchmark risk indicators against which the market-based measure is tested are *a priori* 'better' measures, what is the point of having supervisors paying more attention to the market and imposing indirect market discipline by using market indicators as triggers for prompt corrective action, etc.? On the other hand, if the benchmark indicators are unsatisfactory gauges of risk, what can possibly be learnt from a test where 'success' is defined in terms of a close association between the tested market indicator and the unsatisfactory benchmark measures? Presumably, if markets can track risk as well as accounting ratios or rating agencies do, they might also be able to do it better. If so, failure to uncover any significant relation between the market-based and the benchmark measures is consistent both with the hypothesis that market prices incorporate more information *and* with the hypothesis that they incorporate less information than the benchmark indicators. Event-study-type tests suffer from a similar type of problem, as illustrated by the results of Gropp and Richards (2001), for example.

As should be evident from the brief literature review above, improvements of risk-sensitivity tests have often consisted in controlling for factors thought to influence the extent to which markets can be expected to monitor risk. This reflects a *de facto* recognition that market discipline is conditioned on a number of parameters, such as the institutional setting. However, simply controlling for these factors does not remedy the unobservability problem. In the following section, I outline a method which makes use of the fact that the informativeness of market-based risk indicators is dependent on the *conditions for market discipline*, as laid out in Section 2.1., whereas typical benchmark measures are not (or at least less so). Although the informativeness of different measures cannot be directly observed, observations on the institutional setting can provide a point of reference for inferring the relative informativeness of different risk indicators.

3.   METHOD AND HYPOTHESES

3.1.   Basic setup and hypotheses

Suppose a bank's 'true' risk equals the probability of default P, which is unobserved. There are two types of proxies of P: a market-based indicator, M (e.g. spreads on risky bonds), and a benchmark indicator, B (e.g. accounting informa-

---

[4]   I have not seen this problem explicitly addressed in any of the empirical literature, although the problem is implicit in, e.g., Evanoff and Wall (2001) and Gropp and Richards (2001); already Gorton and Santomero (1990) recognize that the validity of this type of tests is conditional on the auxiliary hypothesis that the independent variables are accurate proxies of true risk; a similar criticism against the approach is raised in Saunders (2001).

tion). A standard 'risk-sensitivity' regression of the market-based risk indicator takes the (simplified) form

$$M = \gamma_0 + \gamma_1 B + w, \tag{1}$$

where w is a random error term. The variance of the error term, var(w), measures how well M proxies B: a small var(w) would suggest that M is a good proxy of B; conversely, a large var(w) would suggest the opposite. It can be shown (see Appendix A) that var(w) can be expressed as a function of two other error variances, var(u) and var(v), which measure, respectively, how accurately M and B proxy P. However, var(u) and var(v) are only 'hypothetical': since we cannot observe P, we cannot actually measure how well M and B proxy it.

One way to describe the unobservability problem is in terms of the contributions of var(u) and var(v) to var(w). We can run the risk-sensitivity regression and observe var(w) (or, strictly speaking, we observe $\hat{w}^2$), but it is not possible to determine the relative contributions of its components. If var(w) is 'large', (i.e., if there is little association between M and B), it could be the consequence both of a large var(u) and of a large var(v). Rejecting the market monitoring hypothesis based on a weak association between M and B effectively entails a *presumption* that var(u) is larger than var(v) (i.e. that B is more informative of P than M is). In fact, we have no way of knowing that this is the case. M could be a poor proxy of B *either* because it is a less informative proxy of P, *or* because it is *more* informative.

Now assume that the informativeness of the market-based indicator depends positively on the extent to which the conditions for market discipline are satisfied, as measured by some variable C_{MD}, whereas the benchmark indicator is invariant to these conditions[5]. In other words, more liquid financial markets, better information, lower bailout probability, etc., will result in a smaller var(u), but will not affect var(v).

Suppose further that from a regression of the type represented by equation (1) over a large sample for which there is 'sufficient' variation in C_{MD}, we retrieve the individual $\hat{w}_i^2$'s. I will call this a measure of the *divergence* between M and B. In line with the above argument, $\hat{w}_i^2$ could be large either because M_i is less informative of P_i than B_i is, or because it is more informative. But we know that the informativeness of M is increasing in C_{MD} (whereas B is invariant to C_{MD}). Now matching each $\hat{w}_i^2$ against the corresponding observation on MD conditions, C_{MDi}, it would make intuitive sense to suggest, for example, that if large $\hat{w}_i^2$'s were observed when conditions for market discipline are poorly satisfied

---

[5]   I will henceforth refer to these conditions as 'conditions for market discipline', 'MD conditions', or sometimes more loosely as 'institutional quality'. The assumption that market-based risk indicators are sensitive to these conditions, whereas common benchmark indicators are not, is qualified and discussed in more detail in subsection 3.2.

(C_{MDi} is 'small'), it is more likely to be because M_i is less informative of P_i than B_i. In fact, it is possible to infer more than that. Suppose that over the entire sample we observe that $\hat{w}_i^2$ consistently decreases as C_{MDi} increases. Such an observation is only consistent with M being an 'initially' less informative indicator of P; as C_{MD} increases, var(u) decreases, thereby also decreasing $\hat{w}_i^2$ – the 'divergence' between M and B. Conversely, if $\hat{w}^2$ consistently *increases* in C_{MD}, then that would suggest that M becomes a poorer and poorer indicator of B – not because it becomes less informative about P (since we know that its informativeness increases in C_{MD}), but because it becomes increasingly *more* informative than B about P[6]. A third possible scenario, of course, is that no significant association is found between $\hat{w}^2$ and C_{MD}. This is most likely to occur if M and B are closely associated, and the errors from the risk-sensitivity regression are small and truly random.

This discussion suggests a two-step methodology, where the overall objective is to infer the difference in informativeness between some market-based and some benchmark indicators of bank risk. The steps are:

1) run a standard risk-sensitivity regression of a market-based risk indicator M on one or several benchmark indicators B. Retrieve the residuals $\hat{w}$, and use them (squared) as a measure of the 'divergence' between M and B;

2) run a regression of $\hat{w}^2$ against some proxy of C_{MD}, and infer the relative informativeness of M and B from the sign of the slope coefficient.

For the second stage regression, the following hypotheses can be formulated with regard to the slope coefficient:

H1. if the market-based indicator M is on average less informative about the true probability of default than the benchmark indicators B, the divergence between M and B (defined as $\hat{w}^2$) will be a decreasing function of MD conditions (the slope coefficient on C_{MD} will be negative). This will be more likely in an institutional setting where the conditions for market discipline are poorly satisfied;

H2. if M is on average more informative than B about the true probability of default, the divergence between M and B will be an increasing function of MD conditions (the slope coefficient on C_{MD} will be positive). This will be more likely for an institutional setting where the conditions for market discipline are well satisfied;

H3. if the market-based indicator M is on average equally informative as the benchmark indicators B, the divergence between M and B will be a zero-slope function of the conditions for market discipline (the slope coefficient

---

[6] Technically, the increase in $\hat{w}_i^2$ is then driven by a decrease in the covariance between u and v, which enters negatively in the equation for var(w), see Appendix A.

on C_{MD} will be small and insignificant). This will (possibly) be more likely in an average-quality institutional setting.

In practice, it is likely that for a large enough sample (sufficient variation in institutional conditions), the relationship between $\hat{w}^2$ and C_{MD} may not be monotonic. In particular, if institutional conditions are bad enough, market prices will not reflect risk as well as other, less 'institution-sensitive' measures do, implying a relatively large divergence; as institutional conditions improve, the gap in informativeness successively closes; ultimately, when institutional conditions are good enough, market prices may increasingly incorporate more information than the benchmark measures, implying that divergence again starts to increase. Therefore, if the benchmark measures are more informative for adverse institutional conditions, but market-based measures are more informative for benevolent institutional conditions, then a non-linear (U-shaped) function should be expected.

To round off this subsection, it is useful to consider more explicitly what testing these hypotheses might actually tell us. First, testing these hypotheses for a sample with a wide enough distribution in MD conditions, the test may inform as to whether market-based risk measures are more informative for some (high) ranges of institutional quality, or, conversely, whether non-market risk measures are more informative for some (low) ranges of institutional quality. By so doing, the test provides a point of reference for assessing the outcome of risk-sensitivity tests of market-based risk indicators in light of the unobservability problem. Second, insofar as the test is devised in a way which allows repeating it for different market-based risk measures and comparing the results, it may inform on the relative informativeness of equity-based risk measures and risk measures based on uninsured debt. Third, the test informs on the relative sensitivity of different market-based measures to MD conditions. These two last issues can contribute to a better understanding of the relative merits of shareholder vs. creditor discipline (for a given institutional setting). All these three aspects contribute to understanding the viability of market discipline in general, and may help to answer questions such as, for example: Is a sub-debt policy a viable alternative to shareholder discipline? Could market discipline (whether by shareholders or creditors) be relied on as a complementary supervisory mechanism even in environments where institutional conditions are relatively poor?

3.2. Discussion

At this point, a few comments on the main assumptions of the methodology described in this section may be warranted. In what follows, I address three key assumptions, point out potential weaknesses, and provide further motivation.

The first discussion relates to the assumption that the benchmark risk measures are invariant to the conditions for market discipline. In theory, these conditions can easily be 'isolated' and defined as distinct vis-à-vis any factors conditioning the informativeness of the benchmark risk measures; in practice, however, the assumption is unlikely to fully hold. To illustrate with an obvious example, the availability of 'good information' should affect the informativeness of market-based risk measures, but is conceivably also strongly correlated with disclosure quality, and therefore with the informativeness of accounting-based benchmark measures. A similar argument could possibly be advanced for other dimensions of MD conditions: factors related to overall financial-system transparency and institutional integrity are likely to positively influence the informativeness of both market-based and benchmark measures of risk.

However, a sufficient condition for the methodology to still be valid is that the market-based measures are *more* responsive to overall MD conditions than the benchmark measures. This is the softer version of the assumption that I effectively rely on in the empirical implementation of the methodology, and it can be motivated by again considering each of the four conditions for market discipline, and their likely impact on the informativeness of market prices on the one hand, and accounting variables on the other[7].

(i)   *open capital markets*: This condition relates to general financial-market efficiency, liquidity, absence of price-distorting restrictions, etc. Almost by definition, it should influence the accuracy of market prices more than the informativeness of accounting variables. It could have an effect on accounting variables as well if financial market development increases the demand for information, and this demand positively affects the quality of financial statements, but if so, the effect is indirect;

(ii)   markets' access to *good information* could, in principle, refer to information from any source, but provided financial statements are an important source of information for financial markets[8], it is clear that – as indicated above – this particular condition for market discipline also measures the informativeness of accounting variables;

(iii) *no prospects of bailout*: this condition directly affects the incentives of an investor to incorporate risk in the price of a financial claim, but it is difficult to see how it should be in any way correlated with disclosure quality;

---

[7] I focus on accounting variables as benchmark indicators here, since that is what I will use in the empirical part of the paper. It is not certain that all arguments are equally applicable to all conceivable kinds of benchmark indicators (e.g. credit ratings).

[8] Yu (2005) finds that accounting transparency significantly affects spreads on corporate bonds – i.e., that bond holders charge an 'opacity premium'; this result would imply that financial statements are an important source of information for investors, and – more indirectly – that the informativeness of (debt) market-based risk indicators and that of accounting-based benchmark indicators are correlated. See also Morgan and Stiroh (2001) for results on the effect of opacity on the risk sensitivity of banks' sub-debt spreads.

(iv) *responsiveness to market signals*: this condition directly measures the 'influence' aspect of market discipline, and could therefore be a determinant of the amount of monitoring effort investors are prepared to expend. Again, it is difficult to see how it should be associated with the informativeness of accounting variables (other than, possibly, via an indirect mechanism related to the information condition [ii]: investors' ability to enforce their interests depends to some extent on the quality of corporate governance, which is in turn associated with the availability of good information).

These considerations seem to suggest that the validity of the assumption that market-based risk indicators are more sensitive to the conditions for market discipline hinges on finding a proxy for these conditions that does not primarily measure condition (ii), but which factors in all four dimensions (or, indeed, focuses on one or all three of the other conditions).

The second assumption up for discussion relates to the possible specification errors in linear risk-sensitivity tests of market-based risk indicators (as mentioned briefly earlier on in the paper). The assumption is that these errors are small and unimportant. Flannery and Sorescu (1996) provide a good overview of possible specification problems for linear bond-spread regressions, but also conclude that the problem of non-linearity is probably small in practice. I effectively rely on this conclusion when specifying the first-stage regressions linearly. The risk I run is that the residuals from these regressions capture a non-linear relationship rather than (or in addition to) differences in informativeness. It is not likely, however, that this would systematically affect the results in the stage-2 regressions. If it does not bias the stage-2 results in any particular direction (which appears difficult to argue), it would simply appear as additional noise which renders estimates somewhat less precise.

A third assumption lies in that the hypotheses developed, and interpretation of the second-stage regression results along the lines I have suggested, presume that the market-based indicator and the benchmark indicators are *ex ante* expected to measure more or less the same thing. It is of course possible that as the conditions for market-based indicators to be informative improve, the divergence between those indicators and the benchmarks could increase because they reflect *different* information better (rather than *more* or *less* information about the same underlying 'true' variable). On the margin, this will probably be the case, to some extent, but I will assume that the effect is not powerful enough to 'crowd out' the effect of differences in informativeness of true risk[9].

---

[9] Assuming anything else would, in fact, imply that most of the empirical literature on market discipline is misspecified from beginning to end.

4. ESTIMATION AND DATA

4.1. Estimation

4.1.1. First-stage regressions

I extract the 'divergence' between three different market-based risk indicators (sub-debt spreads, stock return volatility, and a market version of the so-called Z-score), and a set of benchmark indicators (based on accounting data), for a large panel of banks (see subsection 4.2 for details) by running standard risk-sensitivity regressions. Including period fixed effects in the specification, the risk-sensitivity regression can be reformulated as:

$$m_{it} = \alpha_0 + \alpha_1 D2_i + \ldots + \alpha_{T-1} DT_i + \mathbf{b}_{it}\boldsymbol{\beta} + \mathbf{z}_{it}\boldsymbol{\gamma} + w_{it}, \qquad (2)$$

where m is a market-based indicator of bank risk, $\mathbf{b}$ a vector of benchmark risk indicators, and $\mathbf{z}$ is a vector of control variables[10]. The α_k's represent separate intercepts for each time period between period 1 and period T. This model is estimated by panel least squares on the different market-based risk indicators, and the squared standardized residuals from these regressions are used as measures of the divergence between m and $\mathbf{b}$. There is thus one divergence measure corresponding to each market-based risk measure tested.

4.1.2. Second-stage regressions

The second step consists in running regressions of the divergence measures obtained in step 1 on a proxy for MD conditions. As the primary proxy I use the first principal component of a large number of institutional features (again, see subsection 4.2 for details), denoted *PC1*. In practice, it is not possible to know *a priori* whether the relationship between the divergence measure and the proxy for MD conditions is monotonic or not. Conceivably, for a dataset where the dispersion of observations on the independent variable is sufficiently wide, it would not be – unless, of course, market-based risk measures are not more informative than the benchmark measures for *any* levels of institutional quality actually observed (or, conversely – but perhaps less likely – if market-based risk measures are *always* more informative). Given that a major objective of the paper is to explore this very question – whether market-based risk measures are sometimes 'better' – and given the heterogeneity of the dataset at hand, it is clearly warranted to at least open up for the possibility of a non-monotonic relationship. In order to cover for all eventualities, I will test three different specifications. The first is a simple bivariate linear regression:

---

[10]   See Appendix B for a more formalized description of the estimations, including some technical considerations regarding the use of fixed effects.

$$\hat{w}_{it}^2 = \tau_0 + \tau_1 PC1_{it} + \upsilon_{it} \tag{3}$$

where $\hat{w}_{it}^2$ is the squared standardized residual for the i'th bank at time t, obtained from a regression of equation (2) on one of the considered market-based risk measures, $PC1_{it}$ is the corresponding observation on the first principal component of MD conditions, and υ_{it} is a random error. The second specification is a non-linear version of equation (3):

$$\hat{w}_{it}^2 = \tau_0 + \tau_1 PC1_{it} + \tau_1 PC1_{it}^2 + \upsilon_{it} \tag{4}$$

with notation and variable definitions as above. In some regressions, I will add control variables to the two basic specifications above. Finally, I will run piecewise linear regressions according to the following specification:

$$\hat{w}_{it}^2 = \tau_0 + \tau_1 D_{1it} PC1_{it} + \tau_2 D_{2it} PC1_{it} + \tau_3 D_{3it} PC1_{it} + \tau_4 D_{4it} PC1_{it} + \upsilon_{it} \tag{5}$$

where the D_j's are dummy variables taking on unit value for the first, second, third and fourth quartiles, respectively, of the observations on $PC1$, and zero for all other ranges of $PC1$.

The expectations on the coefficient signs, in line with the hypotheses advanced in subsection 3.1, are as follows. For equation (3), τ_1 will be positive if, on average over the entire sample, the market-based risk measure corresponding to the divergence measure used as dependent variable in the regression is more informative than the benchmark measures (the **b**'s) from equation (2). Conversely, τ_1 will be negative if the benchmark risk measures are more informative on average for the present sample. The final possibility is that τ_1 is insignificantly different from zero, which could have two reasons: first, market and non-market measures may be about equally informative regardless of MD conditions; second, the linear specification is inadequate because the slope coefficient depends on the value of $PC1$ (and positive and negative slopes are more or less symmetrically distributed over $PC1$).

For equation (4), the basic expectation is a convex relationship, implying that τ_2 should be positive, regardless of whether the slope is positive or negative on average. If the relationship is U-shaped, or if a negative effect of mostly inferior market-based measures dominates, then τ_1 should be negative. The perhaps more far-fetched possibility that market-based risk measures are always superior – and increasingly so over the entire range of observations on MD conditions – would imply a positive τ_1.

Finally, the τ_j's from equation (5) can be interpreted in analogy with the τ_1 in equation (3), except now the interpretation is valid only for the sub-sample of $PC1$ corresponding to the τ_j in question. A negative coefficient value would be most expected for τ_1, and a positive value most expected for τ_4.

Equations (3)-(5) are estimated as before by panel OLS, but now without either cross-section or period fixed effects (again, see Appendix B for details).

4.2. Data

The empirical methodology described in the previous section is applied to a panel dataset comprising several hundred banks worldwide. The banks are publicly traded banks with annual financial statement data available in the BankScope database between 1994 and 2005. As data availability varies considerably for different bank-level variables, the exact number of banks covered depends on the combination of variables used in a particular regression specification, but coverage is typically around 300 banks. The bank-specific data is supplemented by country-specific data characterizing various aspects of the institutional setting in the banks' countries of origin (47 countries in all). Appendix C (Tables C1 – C3) provides more detailed information about the sample (in terms of banks, countries, and years covered), and lists all variables used at different stages in the analysis, with brief definitions and sources. In what follows, I describe these variables, explain some of them in more detail, and provide summary statistics.

4.2.1. Market-based risk measures

I use three market-based risk measures, which were chosen on the basis that they were the most frequently used in the literature and/or represented different categories of risk measures (a comprehensive overview of different bank risk measures used in previous literature – whether market-based, accounting-based, or ratings-based – is given in Table D1 in Appendix D).

The first market-based risk measure is the spread over the risk-free interest rate on subordinated notes or bonds. Spreads on sub-debt, or other types of formally uninsured bank debt, have been widely subjected to risk-sensitivity tests of the type represented by equation (2), especially for US data (see the literature review). The spreads used here were observed at year-end and were collected directly from Datastream and Reuters, with comparable risk-free rates subtracted from the sub-debt yields at source. They are mostly secondary-market spreads, but in some cases primary-market spreads were used, depending on availability. A large portion of the banks included did not have any subordinated debt outstanding during the sample period; consequently, subordinated-debt spreads were completely unavailable for these banks. Spreads were also unavailable for a portion of the banks that did have subordinated debt outstanding (according to the balance sheet). As shown in Table 1, the total number of observations on subordinated debt spreads was 637 – considerably less than for the other risk measures. In addition, because accounting data (and consequently benchmark risk measures) are often missing for the early part of the sample period (1994-97) and missing values for sub-debt spreads and accounting variables only partially overlap, about 300 of these observations are lost for the risk-sensitivity regressions.

The second measure is the volatility of total equity returns, which is one of the most widely used equity-based risk measures in the literature[11]. The return volatility is the annualized standard deviation of daily equity returns, calculated separately for each year. Daily stock market prices for the included banks were collected from Datastream.

The third market-based measure is a market version of the so-called Z-score, which is essentially a simplified 'distance to default'. The Z-score is originally defined on accounting variables as

$$Z_{it} = \frac{\mu_{it} + k_{it}}{\sigma_{it}} \qquad (6)$$

where μ_{it} and σ_{it} are the mean and standard deviation, respectively, of bank i's return on assets, and k_{it} is the average share of capital to total assets over the period t. The 'market version' Z-score is calculated using the return on equity and the standard deviation of equity returns. It can be regarded as a combination measure (rather than as a 'pure' market-based measure), since it incorporates both accounting data and stock market data. The Z-score is negatively related to the probability of default (and I therefore use it in the negative as dependent variable for simplicity of comparison)[12].

Summary statistics for the three market-based risk measures appear in Table 1 (panel A). The two equity-based risk measures were divided between bank/year observations where the bank had sub-debt outstanding[13] and observations where it did not, and tested non-parametrically for significant differences in distribution. The purpose of these tests was to provide an initial indication of whether riskier banks are less likely to rely on uninsured debt for financing (as suggested by Covitz et al., 2004), resulting in possible selection bias in risk-sensitivity tests on sub-debt spreads. The results of the tests indicate that there are indeed significant differences in risk between the two groups, although the differences are small. Moreover, the direction of the difference depends on the risk measure used: the stock return volatility measure indicates that banks with sub-debt outstanding are less risky, whereas the Z-score suggests the opposite. These results remain

---

[11] A theoretically 'better' alternative would possibly have been to use the volatility of *abnormal* equity returns, based on some version of the market model or CAPM. I ran several versions of one- and two-factor market models (using Datastream's global general and bank stock price indices), and found that the volatilities of the resulting abnormal returns are correlated with total stock return volatility by a coefficient typically larger than 0.90. I conclude that using one or the other matters little.

[12] The Z-score is widely used as a risk measure in the banking literature, see, e.g., Hannan and Hanweck (1988), Boyd et al. (1993), Beck and Laeven (2006); the market-based version is used by, e.g., Crouzille et al. (2004).

[13] Either because the balance sheet reported a non zero amount of outstanding subordinated debt, or because sub-debt spreads were available for that bank/year observation.

when instead applying a *t*-test to the sub-sample means (not reported). A possible explanation is of course that other factors need to be controlled for; for example, if larger banks are both more likely to issue subordinated debt and more likely to enjoy conjectural government guarantees, then the 'true' relationship between risk and sub-debt issuance likelihood may be obscured in a simple sub-sample comparison.

Table 1. Descriptive statistics, market-based and accounting-based risk measures

The table reports summary statistics for the included market-based (Panel A) and benchmark/accounting-based (Panel B) risk measures. Summary statistics for the included measures (except sub-debt spreads) are reported separately for bank/year observations with subordinated debt outstanding (sub outst.) and those without (no sub outst.), as well as for the full sample of observations (all). The 'Test' column reports the Wilcoxon/Mann-Whitney rank-based test statistic for the null hypothesis that the 'sub outst.' and the 'no sub outst.' groups have equal distributions around the median.

Panel A: Market-based risk measures

	Group	Mean	Std dev	Median	Test	Min	Max	Obs
Sub-debt spread (bp's)	All	115	208	81.0		-370	988	637
Stock return volatility	All	0.0228	0.0171	0.0191		0.000	0.202	4964
	Sub outst.			0.0184				1556
	No sub outst.			0.0196	3.42***			3408
Market Z-score	All	5.35	5.28	3.55		0.350	40.3	2688
	Sub outst.			3.20				1318
	No sub outst.			3.94	8.40***			1370

Panel B. Accounting-based risk measures

	Group	Mean	Std dev	Median	Test	Min	Max	Obs
Leverage	All	0.914	0.055	0.931		0.462	0.990	3322
	Sub outst.			0.942				1510
	No sub outst.			0.914	20.0***			1812
Non-performing loans / equity	All	0.666	0.726	0.458		0.000	4.89	2534
	Sub outst.			0.505				1241
	No sub outst.			0.404	4.74***			1293
Liquid assets / total assets	All	0.253	0.189	0.214		0.000	0.974	3388
	Sub outst.			0.181				1523
	No sub outst.			0.257	8.31***			1865
ROA	All	0.0081	0.0159	0.0077		0.0944	0.0708	3315
	Sub outst.			0.0064				1501
	No sub outst.			0.0090	7.32***			1814

*** Indicates rejection of the null hypothesis of equal medians at the 0.01 level.

4.2.2. Benchmark risk indicators and control variables

The benchmark risk measures used in this paper – as in most of the related literature – are various standard accounting ratios believed to be correlated with the bank's overall risk. A wide range of accounting-based measures have been used, as indicated by Table D1. The categorization of these various measures and the exact choice of variables to be included in the regressions are to some extent a matter of discretion. The vast majority of studies use some measure of leverage, or capitalization. Similarly, different measures of asset structure and/or asset quality are typically included – particularly proxies related to the quality of extended loans and to the ease with which the bank can absorb temporary losses (such as different liquidity measures). Finally, it is common to control for profitability. Based on these conventions, I include *leverage* (defined as one minus the ratio of equity to total assets), *loan quality*, (the ratio of non-performing loans to equity), *liquidity* (liquid assets over total assets), and *the return on assets* (ROA – defined as net earnings divided by total assets)[14].

All these accounting-based benchmark measures are calculated from annual balance sheet and income statement data as reported in BankScope. Descriptive statistics are reported in panel B of Table 1. Again, the sample is divided into subsamples based on whether the bank had subordinated debt outstanding or not. The table reinforces the impression given by the Z-score in the previous table that banks without any outstanding sub-debt are, in fact, *less* risky than other banks. Banks without outstanding sub-debt have significantly lower leverage, lower share of non-performing loans, higher share of liquid assets, and are significantly more profitable than other banks. Again, the conclusion would be that in a heterogeneous sample such as this one, any tendency for riskier banks to be discouraged to issue uninsured debt (if it exists) is obscured by other factors which are more important determinants of sub-debt issuance. Such factors could be related to the size and main line of business of the bank, financial development and other local market conditions, etc. For example, sub-debt issuance is more likely by larger banks, which may benefit from conjectural 'too-big-to-fail' guarantees, and are therefore more risk prone. Another possibility is that subordinated debt is more likely to be issued by banks originating in financial systems that are more developed, less regulated, and more competitive, which could in turn indicate a weaker risk-reducing effect of charter values and lower profitability for these banks (see, e.g., Keeley, 1990; see Boyd and Nicoló, 2005, for an alternative view).

The choice of which control variables to include in the first-stage regressions is a delicate balance, since I want to lose as little information as possible related to the conditions for market discipline, while at the same time controlling for factors unrelated to these conditions. Many of the strongest candidate control variables – such as bank size, ownership structure, home country income level, deposit insurance coverage, etc. (not to mention country dummy variables) – are conceivably strongly correlated with MD conditions. After much deliberation, and loosely following the few previous cross-country studies that exist (see for

---

[14] *Cf.*, e.g., Sironi's (2003) division into a leverage, a profitability, an asset quality, and a liquidity component of bank risk.

instance Angkinand and Wihlborg, 2010), I include three bank-level and four country-level control variables. At the bank level, I include the deposit share of total assets, net interest margin, and the cost/income ratio[15]. These variables are reasonable proxies for general bank characteristics without being too strongly correlated with the extent to which market discipline can be imposed. Moreover, they are fairly orthogonal in variation (a pairwise correlation matrix for the first-stage bank-level variables is shown in Appendix C, Table C4). The source for these, as for previous financial-statement variables, is BankScope. Sub-debt spreads are also controlled for time to maturity (in years) and the size of the issue (the natural logarithm of the issue amount in million USD), in accordance with most previous studies on subordinated debt spreads. This information was collected together with the spreads from the same sources (i.e., Reuters and Datastream).

Table 2. Descriptive statistics, control variables included in first-stage regressions
The table reports summary statistics for the included bank-level and country-level control variables included in the regressions of market-based risk measures on benchmark risk measures.

	Mean	Std dev	Min	Max	Obs
Bank-level control variables					
Deposits	0.82	0.12	0.16	0.95	2878
Net interest margin	0.040	0.051	-0.63	0.48	3363
Cost/income ratio	0.65	0.34	0.077	8.59	3318
Country-level control variables (annual obs's for 47 countries)					
Real interest rate	0.060	0.091	-0.91	0.78	
Inflation	0.067	0.14	-0.039	1.55	
Growth	0.033	0.031	-0.13	0.18	

At the country level, control variables for general macroeconomic conditions are included in the form of the real interest rate, the inflation rate, and real GDP growth – all from the World Bank's *World Development Indicators*. To control for the possibility that a systemic financial crisis (such as the Asian financial crisis in 1997-98 or the Argentinean bank crisis in 2001) has an independent effect on the extent to which different risk measures diverge, I include a crisis dummy. The

---

[15]   The one control variable that is included in almost all previous studies on bank risk is the size of the bank (typically measured as the log of total assets). Most of my deliberations revolved around whether to include this variable or not in the first-stage regressions. Absolute bank size would be correlated with the extent to which market discipline can be imposed insofar as it proxies for the existence of conjectural 'too-big-to-fail' guarantees, and for general liquidity of the bank's stock and bonds. These aspects of MD conditions should obviously be (and are) accounted for in the second-stage regressions. Therefore, because of the substantial risk that 'bank size'– in the absence of more direct proxies – would pick up a lot of these dimensions of MD conditions (with the effect that much information is lost for the second stage of the analysis), I decided in the end *not* to include bank size as a control variable.

source for identifying countries/years where there was a systemic crisis was Honohan and Laeven (2005) and Laeven and Valencia (2008).

4.2.3. Proxies of the conditions for market discipline

As the primary measure of MD conditions I use the first principal component of a set of bank- and country-level variables – each of which proxy for one dimension or other of the extent to which the conditions for market discipline are satisfied. A relatively large number of bank-level and firm-level variables were used to construct the composite measure. Variable definitions are summarized in Table C3 (Panel B), with indicative categorizations according to which one of Lane's (1993) four conditions for market discipline that they primarily capture, as well as brief descriptions where definitions are not obvious. Summary statistics are reported in Table 3. The exact choice of variables contains an obvious discretionary element, but because the data are reduced, the choice is a matter of trading off tractability and comprehensiveness, rather than a matter of accuracy in capturing any one specific condition for market discipline.

The data reduction itself has advantages and drawbacks. The motive for using principal components analysis (and for focusing on the first principal component) in this paper is essentially three-fold. First, for ease of interpretation, it is preferable to focus on *one* proxy of C_{MD}, which however by definition is a multi-dimensional concept. Reducing the data makes it possible to capture several facets of the concept in a single measure. Second, the technique implies 'efficient' use of the variation in individual proxies of MD conditions, and avoidance of multicollinearity issues due to high correlation between (some of) these individual proxies. Third, the variation in the individual variables used to proxy C_{MD} occurs at the bank-level for some variables, at the country level for others; combining them eliminates the need to deal with potential interpretation and error-correction problems associated with this partial 'clustering' of the data. A potential drawback with the method is that one potentially loses sight of the contribution of specific dimensions of MD conditions, or specific market-discipline conditions[16]. A related problem is caused by the fact that the principal components are orthogonal to one another. This makes it increasingly difficult to interpret the (successively less important) higher-order components in terms of what they have to say about the overall conditions for market discipline.

---

[16] Suppose, for instance, we are particularly interested in analyzing the extent to which deposit insurance coverage contributes to making spreads on subordinated bonds a more or less informative measure of bank risk. Insofar as the proxy for deposit insurance coverage is decomposed according to its (partial) covariation with other measures of MD conditions, and the principal components are aggregations of different measures, this contribution may be difficult to assess.

Below follows a description by category of the variables that went into the principal components analysis.

(i)   *open capital markets:* This condition for market discipline is primarily captured by a proxy of the liquidity of the bank's securities (the average daily turnover rate of the bank's stock), and various standard measures of financial development at country level. I used four measures suggested by Rajan and Zingales (2003) – total bank deposits (or M2, as available) over GDP, stock market capitalization over GDP, net equity issues over gross fixed capital formation, and the number of firms with stock traded on public exchanges per million of population; in addition, I used private sector credit over GDP (as suggested by La Porta *et al.*, 1997), and private sector bond market capitalization as a share of GDP. Sources for these variables were IMF *International Financial Statistics* or the World Bank's *World Development Indicators* (GDP, investment, bank deposits, and credit); Eurostat (stock market capitalization for most European countries) or Datastream (all other stock market data); and the Bank for International Settlements (bond market capitalization). Net equity issues were proxied as the year-on-year change in stock market capitalization, corrected for the change in stock prices as measured by Datastream's overall market price index for each country. Net issues were calculated for each of the years 1994-2005, and then averaged. To capture the international dimension of capital market openness, finally, I used an index of foreign-investment openness, based on the presence of restrictions on capital-account transactions as reported in the IMF's *Annual Report on Exchange Arrangements and Exchange Restrictions*, and taken from Brune *et al.* (2001);

(ii)   *quality of information:* The availability of bank-specific information is proxied by a single country-level index variable. The variable equals CIFAR's index of overall financial-reporting transparency (see Bushman *et al.*, 2004) for all countries where this index is available, and Barth *et al.*'s (2001, 2006) private monitoring index (recalculated to the CIFAR scale) for all other countries[17];

(iii)   *no prospects of being bailed out:* The probability that claimants on the bank will be bailed out depends primarily on explicit and implicit deposit insurance coverage. As a proxy for the share of formally insured debt (at the bank level), I use country-level data on the fraction of deposit value covered by explicit deposit insurance (net of the coinsurance ratio; available from

---

[17]   It is clear that the focus on accounting transparency in this condition for market discipline makes it questionable whether market-based risk measures are more responsive to the condition than the accounting-based benchmark measures. However, as argued in Section 3, a sufficient condition for the paper's main hypotheses to hold is that market-based measures are *more* responsive to the *overall* conditions for market discipline than the benchmarks; if the market-based measure and the accounting-based measure are about equally responsive to financial-statement transparency (as seems plausible), the inclusion of this variable neither adds nor subtracts anything from the end results. Conceivable alternative measures of quality of information typically make use of the market variables themselves (as in Morck *et al.*, 2000, and Durnev *et al.*, 2003, for instance).

Demirgüç-Kunt *et al.*, 2005), and multiply it by the ratio of deposits to total debt for each bank and year. For countries where a specific coverage percentage is not available, I use $\min\left(1, \dfrac{\text{coverage limit}}{\text{deposits/capita}}\right)$ – coinsurance ratio as a proxy (also from Demirgüç-Kunt *et al.*, 2005), and multiply by the ratio of deposits to total debt for each bank and year, as previously. The share of formally insured debt is always zero for countries/years with no explicit deposit insurance scheme.

Implicit guarantees are proxied by a variable called 'no-bailout credibility' in Table C3. It equals the Fitch Support Rating (which is an index variable showing the probability that a bank will be bailed out in case of default) for banks where such a rating is available; for all other banks, I take one less the bank's share of total deposits in its country of origin and transform the result to the Fitch scale. Balance-sheet data on deposits for each bank and data on total deposits (or M2) in each country are from BankScope and IMF's *International Financial Statistics*, respectively, as before. Finally, I use the Reuters ownership data (see under condition [iv], below) to construct a government-ownership dummy, to account for the possibility that government-owned banks may be more likely to be bailed out in the event of failure;

(iv) *responsiveness to market signals:* The last condition for market discipline is summarized at the bank level by a number of corporate governance variables (in the absence of more direct proxies for responsiveness). Ownership data were collected from Reuters. The Reuters database distinguishes between ownership by three types of owner: insiders/stakeholders, institutions, and mutual funds. It contains percentages of ownership by the different categories and by individual shareholders within the three groups. Both insider ownership and outsider ownership (as proxied by the ownership share of institutional investors) were used. In addition, responsiveness to market signals may depend on how well capitalized the bank is. To measure this in a simple way, the minimum Tier-1 capital requirement (assumed to be 50% of the home country's total capital requirement, as reported by Barth *et al.*, 2001, 2006) is subtracted from each bank's equity-to-assets ratio; the result gives the proxy for 'excess capital'. At the country level, bank claimants' possibilities to exert influence are proxied by the widely used creditor and shareholder rights indices (originally from La Porta *et al.*, 1997, 1998; with additional country scores from Allen *et al.*, 2006; Djankov *et al.*, 2007, 2008; and Pistor *et al.*, 2000), and the *International Country Risk Guide*'s index of legal system integrity.

Table 3. Descriptive statistics, conditions for market discipline

The table reports summary statistics for variables included in the composite measures of the extent to which the conditions for market discipline are satisfied (open capital markets, good information, no prospects of bailout, and responsiveness to market signals).

	Mean	Std dev	Min	Max	Obs
Bank-level variables					
Turnover rate	0.79	2.27	0.00	53.3	4564
Share of formally insured debt	0.53	0.35	0.00	0.99	2881
No-bailout credibility	3.56	1.45	1.00	5.00	5066
Institutional ownership	0.10	0.16	0.00	0.98	5377
Insider ownership	0.39	0.31	0.00	0.99	5377
Excess capital	0.044	0.055	-0.030	0.49	3322
Country-level variables (annual obs's for 47 countries)					
Bank deposits/GDP	0.67	0.36	0.10	2.55	
Private-sector credit/GDP	0.84	0.63	0.072	2.60	
Equity issues/Gross Fixed Capital Formation	0.18	0.13	0.021	0.63	
Equity market capitalization/GDP	0.45	0.40	0.00	2.75	
Number of publicly traded firms/mn. population	23.3	28.5	1.13	194	
Corporate bond market capitalization/GDP	0.31	0.40	0.00	2.12	
Foreign-investment openness	3.51	2.71	0.00	9.00	
Corporate transparency/private monitoring index	67.2	8.74	32.7	85.0	
Shareholder rights index	3.16	1.25	1.00	5.00	
Creditor rights index	2.39	1.24	0.00	4.00	
Index of rule of law	4.15	1.38	1.00	6.00	

Table 4 reports a summary of the outcome of the principal components analysis on all the variables described above. I have only included the first six principal components in Table 4 (as well as in the stage-two regressions), as higher-order components account for less than five percent each of the variation in the proxies for MD conditions. The proportion of the total variance accounted for by each of components 1-6 is shown in Panel A in the table. The first component – that on which I mainly rely – explains about 28 percent of the variation. The first six components together account for about 70 percent of the variation in the variables described previously in this sub-section.

Panel B of Table 4 reports the coefficients of the individual market discipline conditions for principal components 1-6. It shows that the first principal component, $PC1$, puts most weight on the indicators of financial system development, but is also strongly positively correlated with the quality of information (the transparency index), and general legal-system integrity (as proxied by the rule-of-law index). The one dimension of MD conditions that is not well reflected in $PC1$ is the no-bailout condition. This dimension is instead an important element in the second principal component, $PC2$ – as indicated by the positive coefficient on 'no-bailout credibility' and the negative (though relatively small) weights on the share of formally insured debt and government ownership. *PC2* seems however to be negatively related to the responsiveness dimension of MD conditions (as indicated by the positive coefficient on 'excess capital' and the negative one on the shareholder rights index). This illustrates the point made earlier that higher-order principal components become increasingly more difficult to interpret in terms of their *overall* impact on the conditions for market discipline. This point is further reinforced by looking at coefficients for *PC3-PC6*. It is not always clear whether the 'net' impact of these components on general MD conditions is positive or negative. Due to this difficulty of interpretation, *PC2-PC6* will only be used as control variables in the regressions on the divergence measures to check the stability of the estimates on the first principal component (rather than as explanatory variables in their own right).

Table 4. Principal components analysis of conditions for market discipline, summary
Panel A reports eigenvalues and variance proportions of the first six principal components (of a total of 18 components) from a principal components analysis on the conditions for market discipline, based on the correlation matrix of the included variables. *PC1* refers to the first principal component, *PC2* to the second, etc. The bottom row in Panel A shows cumulative variance proportions. Panel B shows coefficients on the individual proxies of the conditions for market discipline. The total number of included observations was 1862.

Panel A. Eigenvalues and variance proportions						
	PC1	PC2	PC3	PC4	PC5	PC6
Eigenvalue	4.96	2.37	1.70	1.38	1.23	0.99
Variance proportion	0.275	0.131	0.095	0.077	0.068	0.055
Cumulative variance proportion	0.275	0.407	0.502	0.578	0.647	0.702

Panel B. Coefficients of individual proxies of MD conditions						
	PC1	PC2	PC3	PC4	PC5	PC6
Open capital markets						
Turnover rate	-0.08	0.04	-0.21	0.07	-0.49	0.42
Bank deposits/GDP	0.29	-0.31	0.17	-0.04	0.04	0.35
Private-sector credit/GDP	0.33	0.02	0.36	0.01	0.01	0.16
Equity issues/Gross Fixed Capital Formation	0.24	-0.24	-0.27	-0.39	0.00	0.17
Equity market capitalization/GDP	0.38	-0.06	-0.03	-0.25	0.04	0.13
Number of publicly traded firms/mn. population	0.31	-0.15	-0.35	0.06	0.13	0.07
Corporate bond market capitalization/GDP	0.24	0.45	0.13	0.11	0.05	0.03
Foreign-investment openness	0.32	0.29	-0.05	-0.08	0.08	0.08
Good information						
Corporate transparency/private monitoring index	0.33	0.08	-0.03	0.16	0.12	-0.11
No prospects of bailout						
Share of formally insured debt	-0.02	-0.07	0.64	-0.03	-0.28	0.23
No-bailout credibility	-0.04	0.38	-0.11	-0.03	0.27	0.00
Government ownership	-0.12	-0.19	-0.07	0.26	0.40	0.43

Responsiveness to market signals						
Insider ownership	-0.23	-0.07	0.01	-0.42	0.28	0.18
Institutional ownership	0.14	-0.13	-0.27	0.22	-0.51	-0.08
Excess capital	-0.03	0.35	-0.26	-0.22	-0.18	0.23
Shareholder rights index	0.10	-0.42	-0.04	0.21	0.11	-0.30
Creditor rights index	-0.14	0.07	-0.10	0.54	0.15	0.42
Index of rule of law	0.34	0.13	0.08	0.22	0.02	-0.08

5.   RESULTS

5.1. First-stage regressions

Table 5 reports the results of the first-stage regressions on all three market-based indicators. Coefficient columns 1 and 2 report the results for two specifications of the regressions on sub-debt spreads, where the only difference is that model (2) includes a correction term for possible selection bias (which was constructed because the summary statistics suggested a significant difference in risk distribution for the sub-sample of banks that had issued sub-debt vis-à-vis those banks that had not). I followed Covitz *et al.* (2004), Birchler and Hancock (2004), and Evanoff and Jagtiani (2004), and adopted the Heckman (1979) two-step approach to selection-bias correction, where the correction term is the inverse Mills ratio from a probit regression on a dummy variable indicating whether or not a bank had issued sub-debt for each period. To preserve space, and because they are of secondary interest for the main analysis, the specification and results of this regression are reported in Appendix C (Table C6). As evident from Table 5, selection bias seems to be a minor issue here, and the inclusion of the correction term does not affect the overall results. (I therefore use the squared standardized residuals from model [1] as the sub-debt spread divergence measure in the second-stage regressions.)

All benchmark risk measures except leverage significantly influence sub-debt spreads, whereas the common control variables have little effect. In terms of coefficient signs, the (negative) market Z-score responds in a similar way as the sub-debt spread, whereas stock return volatility coefficients on both leverage and ROA are negative (but indistinguishable from zero). Both equity-based measures are much more sensitive to variation in the macroeconomy (except to real interest rates).

In line with the implications of the unobservability problem and the fact that the regressions deliberately leave out variables believed to influence the estimated relationships, I do not want to draw too far-reaching conclusions from these first-stage results. I just observe that they seem, overall, fully reconcilable with results reached in previous studies using similar approaches and specifications (e.g., Sironi, 2003, for a cross-country sample of sub-debt spreads, and Hall *et al.*, 2004, for various stock-market measures of risk, using US data).

Table 5. Results of regressions of market-based risk measures on accounting-based risk measures

The table reports coefficient estimates from panel OLS regressions with period fixed effects. T-statistics in parentheses are based on White type standard errors robust to time-varying residual variance and correlation over time within cross-sections. In the regressions on sub-debt spreads, accounting variables and macroeconomic variables are measured in percent (rather than fractions). Market Z-score is entered negatively in the regression (it decreases in risk) for ease of comparability. Squared standardized residuals from regressions 1, 3, and 4 are used as 'divergence' measures (for sub-debt, stock return volatility, and Z-score, respectively) in the subsequent analysis.

	Dependent variable			
	1. Sub-debt spread	2. Sub-debt spread	3. Stock return volatility	4. Negative market Z-score
Leverage	12.2 (1.08)	10.9 (0.96)	-0.019 (-1.40)	48.9 (6.72)***
Non-performing loans	1.20 (2.03)**	1.21 (2.02)**	0.004 (5.27)***	0.76 (3.64)***
Liquid assets	3.00 (1.91)*	3.01 (1.91)*	0.024 (5.97)***	3.98 (4.66)***
Return on assets (ROA)	60.9 (2.19)**	63.8 (2.27)**	-0.028 (-0.55)	4.08 (0.33)
Time to maturity	-3.78 (-2.58)**	-3.82 (-2.61)***		
Amount of issue	-15.3 (-0.73)	-16.8 (-0.78)		
Heckman 'lambda'[a]		-22.1 (-0.68)		
Deposits	0.072 (0.054)	0.29 (0.22)	-0.003 (-0.50)	-0.91 (-0.73)
Net interest margin	-3.54 (-0.32)	-3.89 (-0.34)	-0.051 (-3.22)***	-21.5 (-2.69)***
Cost/income ratio	-0.15 (-0.098)	-0.27 (-0.18)	0.001 (0.28)	-0.86 (-1.50)
Real interest rate	2.14 (1.04)	2.15 (1.06)	0.013 (1.62)	5.75 (3.79)***
Inflation	15.7 (1.34)	15.3 (1.30)	0.047 (6.72)***	12.4 (5.03)***
Growth	21.4 (1.87)*	19.14 (1.67)*	0.035 (2.71)***	21.3 (5.08)***
Systemic financial crisis	38.5 (0.87)	35.8 (0.79)	0.004 (3.12)***	1.56 (4.73)***
Period fixed effects (F-statistic)	5.18***	5.28***	9.32***	4.80***
Adj. R2	0.33	0.33	0.26	0.33
Regression F	7.55***	7.26***	35.5***	47.7***
No. of observations	267	264	1831	1781
No. of banks	97	96	349	347

*/**/*** denotes significance at 10/5/1 percent confidence level.
Note: a) Correction for possible selection bias, based on the Heckman (1979) two-step procedure; the variable is the inverse Mills ratio calculated from a probit selection regression, as specified in Table 6.

5.2. Second-stage regressions

5.2.1. Sub-debt spread divergence

Table 6 reports the stage-two results for sub-debt spread divergence (i.e., the squared standardized residuals from the stage-one regressions on sub-debt spreads). Five different specifications are estimated, all using different combinations of the first six principal components of MD conditions as independent variables. The first coefficient column shows sub-debt spread divergence regressed on an intercept and the first principal component of MD conditions only. It indicates a positive average relationship, but the right-hand-side variables are jointly insignificant, as indicated by the regression F-statistic. Controlling for principal components 2 through 6, the slope coefficient on the first component proves to be negative on average for the whole sample (specification [2]).

Models (3) and (4) are specified to reflect the hypothesis of a possible non-monotonic relationship between divergence and MD conditions. They allow for a second-degree polynomial relationship between the divergence measure and the first principal component of MD conditions – with or without controlling (linearly) for components 2-6. These specifications – especially model (4) – seem to strongly suggest a U-shaped relationship between divergence in information content and institutional quality, very much in accordance with the hypotheses advanced. In other words, as the institutional conditions for market discipline move from poor to average, the divergence between sub-debt spreads and the accounting-based risk measures becomes successively smaller (indicating that accounting-based indicators are initially 'better' when conditions are poor); but as conditions continue to improve, divergence starts to increase again (suggesting that the informativeness of sub-debt spreads is higher than that of accounting variables when conditions are good). The piecewise specification, finally, strongly supports the results of the non-linear specifications. The slope on the independent variable is significantly negative for the first two quartiles of $PC1$, zero for the third, and significantly positive for the top quartile.

In line with what has been said earlier about the composition of higher-order principal components, I have made no attempt to interpret the coefficients on $PC2$-$PC6$ in specifications (2) and (4). They are entered only as a means to check the stability of the estimates on $PC1$. Overall, these seem reasonably stable qualitatively, in the sense that they are consistent with a convex relationship between sub-debt spread divergence and $PC1$, which is negative on average over the full sample distribution of $PC1$, but turns positive toward the end of this distribution.

Table 6. Results of regressions of sub-debt spread divergence on conditions for market discipline

The table reports coefficient estimates from panel OLS regressions of the squared standardized residual from model 1 in Table 5 on various combinations of the first six principal components of the conditions for market discipline (PC1-PC6). Model 5 reports coefficient estimates from a piecewise linear regression on the first principal component, where the distribution of the independent variable is split into four even quartiles. T-statistics in parentheses are based on White standard errors robust to contemporaneous correlation and cross-section heteroscedasticity.

	1	2	3	4	5
Intercept	0.88 (4.90)***	0.74 (4.51)***	0.36 (2.29)**	0.31 (2.11)**	0.37 (2.02)**
PC1	0.11 (4.60)***	-0.11 (-4.00)***	-0.005 (-0.17)	-0.13 (-5.71)***	
PC1^2			0.11 (24.5)***	0.10 (10.9)***	
PC2		-0.17 (-2.31)**		-0.11 (-1.57)	
PC3		-0.24 (-7.73)***		0.043 (1.13)	
PC4		0.080 (1.45)		0.13 (2.31)**	
PC5		-0.42 (-3.35)***		-0.41 (-3.36)***	
PC6		-0.17 (-1.98)**		-0.21 (-2.03)**	
PC1 – Q1					-0.25 (-3.55)***
PC1 – Q2					-0.38 (-3.83)***
PC1 – Q3					0.03 (0.31)
PC1 – Q4					0.43 (12.14)***
Adj. R^2	0.01	0.06	0.06	0.09	0.06
Regression F	2.40	3.71***	8.87***	4.36***	4.66***
No. of observations	239	239	239	239	239
No. of banks	91	91	91	91	91

*/**/*** denotes significance at 10/5/1 percent confidence level.

Although the overall explanatory power is fairly low for these regressions (as expected), these results would suggest that the unobservability problem cannot be ignored in risk-sensitivity tests of sub-debt spreads in relatively mature markets with limited implicit guarantees of formally uninsured bank liabilities. This result seems to open up for an alternative interpretation of the 'non-results' of, e.g., Hall *et al.* (2004), Covitz *et al.* (2004), and Krishnan *et al.* (2006). They all find, by and large, that standard benchmark measures of banks' default risk are not significantly reflected in the spreads of risky debt, and interpret the results in terms of a lack of risk-sensitivity on the part of the market-based measure. The point of the unobservability problem is that this interpretation cannot be made, unless we are certain that the benchmark indicator is *always* more informative (which, in turn, disqualifies much of the idea with market discipline in the first place). The results reported here on the relationship between sub-debt spread divergence and the conditions for market discipline suggest that the lack of risk-sensitivity may be on the part of the benchmark measures, rather than on sub-debt spreads.

5.2.2. Stock return volatility divergence

Table 7 shows the results of estimation of stock return volatility divergence as a function of the principal components of MD conditions. Here, too, the results support the supposition of an initially negative but convex function. The slope coefficients on the first principal component are consistently negative. Allowing for a non-linear relationship, the coefficient for the quadratic term turns out significantly positive (but small). Controlling for successively less important principal components does little to boost explanatory power, and does not affect the coefficients of $PC1$ and $PC1^2$.

Finally, the results of the piecewise specification, as reported in coefficient column (5), support the results of the non-linear specifications (3) and (4) for all but the bottom 25 percent of MD conditions. For quartiles 2-4, the coefficients on the first principal component are all negative and significant, but decrease in magnitude as conditions for market discipline improve. For the top quartile, the coefficient is close to zero, indicating that the divergence between stock return volatility and the accounting benchmark measures is relatively insensitive to improvements in MD conditions for this sub-sample; however, the coefficient is still significantly negative, so there is no basis for suggesting that stock-return volatility contain more information on bank risk for higher levels of institutional development (as was the case with sub-debt spreads). The coefficient for the bottom fourth of $PC1$ is insignificantly different from zero. In line with the basic hypotheses and arguments advanced previously, this would suggest that the difference in information quality between the stock-market indicator and the accounting indicators is random when market-discipline conditions are poorly satisfied. A tentative explanation for this finding is that both types of indicator are 'just as bad' when the institutional environment is sufficiently poor. This explanation conflicts somewhat with the assumption that the benchmark measures are invariant to MD conditions, but it would seem to be the most plausible explanation for this result.

Notwithstanding the indeterminate result for the first quartile in specification (5), the overall impression from all regressions reported in Table 7 is that the divergence between stock return volatility and accounting risk is a negative function of the conditions for market discipline, but that the negative slope becomes increasingly flat as conditions improve. The implication is that accounting measures of risk are *a priori* more informative, but the difference in informativeness becomes successively less important.

Table 7. Results of regressions of stock return volatility divergence on conditions for market discipline

The table reports coefficient estimates from panel OLS regressions of the squared standardized residual from model 3 in Table 5 on various combinations of the first six principal components of the conditions for market discipline (PC1-PC6). Model 5 reports coefficient estimates from a piecewise linear regression on the first principal component, where the distribution of the independent variable is split into four even quartiles. T-statistics in parentheses are based on White standard errors robust to contemporaneous correlation and cross-section heteroscedasticity.

	1	2	3	4	5
Intercept	0.60 (7.80)***	0.62 (7.23)***	0.52 (7.20)***	0.51 (6.29)***	0.49 (5.09)***
PC1	-0.14 (-4.07)***	-0.13 (-4.04)***	-0.14 (-4.27)***	-0.13 (-4.34)***	
PC1^2			0.017 (4.42)***	0.022 (2.42)**	
PC2		0.060 (2.56)**		0.074 (2.55)**	
PC3		-0.015 (-0.83)		0.035 (0.95)	
PC4		0.080 (1.45)		-0.039 (-2.12)**	
PC5		-0.053 (-2.34)**		0.050 (4.56)***	
PC6		0.10 (3.09)***		0.084 (2.41)**	
PC1 – Q1					-0.071 (-1.27)
PC1 – Q2					-0.24 (-3.01)***
PC1 – Q3					-0.13 (-2.47)**
PC1 – Q4					-0.043 (-2.71)***
Adj. R^2	0.03	0.03	0.03	0.04	0.04
Regression F	47.0***	9.49***	25.7***	8.88***	15.0***
No. of observations	1489	1489	1489	1489	1489
No. of banks	282	282	282	282	282

*/**/*** denotes significance at 10/5/1 percent confidence level.

5.2.3. Z-score divergence

The results from regressions of Z-score divergence on the conditions for market discipline (Table 8) impart the overall impression of a monotonically increasing divergence between the Z-score and the accounting-based benchmarks over the entire distribution of MD conditions. The first principal component of the conditions for market discipline has a consistently positive and highly significant coefficient for specifications (1)-(4). The quadratic PC1 terms in specifications (3) and (4), on the other hand, are small and statistically insignificant. The piecewise specification on the first principal component, finally, seems to suggest that divergence increases the most over low-to-medium ranges of MD conditions, but the parameter estimates for this specification are jointly insignificant (as shown by the regression F).

The overall insignificance of specification (5), along with the very small R^2's in specifications (1) and (3), suggests that the first principal component explains considerably less of the Z-score divergence than the divergence of stock return volatility and sub-debt spreads. The higher-order principal components ($PC2$-$PC6$), on the other hand, seem to add considerably to the explanatory power of the regressions (without necessarily clarifying the relationship between Z-score divergence and overall MD conditions).

The implication of the results – in accordance with the hypotheses laid out in this paper – would be that the Z-score is always more informative on bank risk than accounting-based risk indicators. However, given the relatively low capacity of the most overall measure of MD conditions (*viz.* the first principal component) to explain this difference in informativeness, the message needs perhaps to be nuanced somewhat.

One explanation could lie in the fact that the Z-score is a combination measure, incorporating both market and accounting data. Keeping this in mind, a possible implication of the result could run along the lines that combination measures capture information not contained in more one-dimensional measures of risk, and the market can always produce valuable complementary information (regardless of the level of institutional quality).

This line of interpretation would suggest that the results here obtained substantiate the results of previous research – by, e.g., Berger *et al.* (2000), Evanoff and Wall (2001), Gunther *et al.* (2001), and Gropp *et al.* (2006) – which has also concluded that information impounded in market measures of risk could provide an important complementary signal of banks' financial health, and thus has pointed to the potential value of indirect market discipline in bank supervision.

Table 8. Results of regressions of market Z-score divergence on conditions for market discipline

The table reports coefficient estimates from panel OLS regressions of the squared standardized residual from model 4 in Table 5 on various combinations of the first six principal components of the conditions for market discipline (PC1-PC6). Model 5 reports coefficient estimates from a piecewise linear regression on the first principal component, where the distribution of the independent variable is split into four even quartiles. T-statistics in parentheses are based on White standard errors robust to contemporaneous correlation and cross-section heteroscedasticity.

	1	2	3	4	5
Intercept	0.78 (7.25)***	0.96 (6.01)***	0.85 (4.17)***	0.95 (4.69)***	0.82 (4.30)***
PC1	0.086 (2.90)***	0.15 (3.21)***	0.082 (2.25)**	0.15 (2.88)***	
PC1^2			-0.014 (-0.58)	0.001 (0.042)	
PC2		0.63 (3.58)***		0.63 (3.59)***	
PC3		-0.047 (-1.01)		-0.045 (-0.94)	
PC4		-0.041 (-0.39)		-0.040 (-0.41)	
PC5		0.13 (2.41)**		0.13 (2.15)**	
PC6		0.26 (6.48)***		0.26 (7.66)***	
PC1 – Q1					0.10 (2.11)**
PC1 – Q2					0.13 (2.16)**
PC1 – Q3					0.13 (0.80)
PC1 – Q4					-0.000 (-0.002)
Adj. R^2	0.003	0.06	0.002	0.06	0.002
Regression F	4.65**	17.7***	2.75*	15.1***	1.62
No. of observations	1483	1483	1483	1483	1483
No. of banks	282	282	282	282	282

*/**/*** denotes significance at 10/5/1 percent confidence level.

5.2.4. Regressions on individual conditions for market discipline

As an additional robustness test of the results, and as a means to clarify the results, I ran regressions of the three divergence measures extracted from the stage-one regressions on an individual proxy of the conditions of market discipline. The proxy used as regressor in these additional stage-two regressions is the 'no-bailout credibility' variable. It was chosen on the grounds that it is a bank-level variable, has a low weight in the first principal component of MD conditions (and thus so far 'untested'), and has a relatively 'clean' interpretation in terms of its impact on the viability of market-based measures of risk. I ran one linear and one quadratic specification for each divergence measure (equivalent to specifications [1] and [3] in Tables 6-8). The results are reported in Table 9.

Table 9. Regressions on individual conditions for market discipline

The table reports coefficient estimates from panel OLS regressions of the squared standardized residuals from model 1 (sub-debt spread divergence), model 3 (stock-return volatility divergence), and model 4 (Z-score divergence) in Table 5 on an index of 'no-bailout credibility'. T-statistics in parentheses are based on White standard errors robust to contemporaneous correlation and cross-section heteroscedasticity.

	Dependent variable					
	Sub-debt spread divergence		Stock-return volatility divergence		Z-score divergence	
	1	2	1	2	1	2
Intercept	1.77 (6.06)***	3.50 (6.06)***	0.04 (0.17)	-0.18 (-0.28)	-0.84 (-3.27)***	1.81 (5.65)***
No-bailout credibility	-0.29 (-5.56)***	-1.80 (-5.58)***	0.26 (3.30)***	0.42 (0.72)	0.51 (4.58)***	-1.47 (-4.85)***
(No-bailout credibility)^2		0.25 (5.33)***		-0.02 (-0.26)		0.30 (4.86)***
Adj. R^2	0.03	0.05	0.004	0.004	0.02	0.03
Regression F	8.18***	7.89***	8.58***	4.32**	42.2***	28.6***
No. of obs.	259	259	1823	1823	1773	1773
No. of banks	96	96	348	348	346	346

*/**/*** denotes significance at 10/5/1 percent confidence level.

Sub-debt spread divergence displays a negative average relationship with no-bailout credibility, but when the quadratic term is introduced again proves to be a convex function, in accordance both with the hypotheses advanced and with the results obtained earlier when the first principal component was used as regressor. The estimated relationship suggests that sub-debt spread divergence drops for the initial two thirds of the distribution of no-bailout credibility, but then bottoms out and turns positive for the top third of the distribution. The function hits its minimum at around 3.5, which is close to the mean value for no-bailout credibility.

Stock return volatility divergence instead shows a positive overall relationship with no-bailout credibility, but as indicated by the very low adjusted R^2's and the insignificance of all regressors in the quadratic specification, the association is relatively weak. The conclusion would be that this particular dimension of the conditions for market discipline is less important than those dimensions captured in the first principal components.

Z-score divergence, finally, appears to be positively related to no-bailout credibility on average, but allowing for non-linearity, the posited convex relationship emerges. The estimated coefficients in specification (2) for Z-score divergence are similar to those estimated for sub-debt spread divergence, although the function reaches its minimum somewhat earlier (which explains why the estimated relationship is positive on average). Comparing these results with those obtained with the first principal component of MD conditions as the primary explanatory variable, it is clear that the no-bailout condition has a higher power to explain the difference in informativeness between the Z-score and accounting variables than those proxies of MD conditions that have a high weight in $PC1$.

Again, a possible explanation of the finding that the Z-score more often has a higher informativeness than the benchmark indicators is that it incorporates information contained in both market prices and accounting data. These two types of information could be complementary even when the institutional environment is not good enough to make market-based measures *individually* 'better' than accounting-based indicators of bank risk.

6. CONCLUSIONS

The potential merits of market discipline in banking have often been assessed empirically by focusing on the monitoring aspect of market discipline – that is, the extent to which prices on banks' securities reflect the risk of the issuing banking organization. Two main approaches have been adopted: the 'risk sensitivity' approach (where various indicators of risk derived from market prices are regressed on benchmark risk measures, such as different accounting ratios, or credit ratings), and the 'early warning' approach (where market-based risk measures are tested as predictors, or leading indicators, of bank distress, defined in some way). The overall results are relatively inconclusive, and each approach has its methodological problems. I have focused on the former approach in this paper. In this approach, one previously largely overlooked problem is that both market-based risk measures and the benchmark indicators commonly used are imperfect proxies of 'true' risk. Therefore, absence of a significant association between a market signal and benchmark risk indicators could result either because market prices do not adequately reflect risk, or because market prices in fact incorporate the available information on banks' risk *better* than other available measures.

The problem is thus that it is not possible to observe which of the indicators that is more informative about the bank's 'true' risk. What *is* possible to observe, though, is how well the institutional setting in a particular market is geared toward inducing market discipline. In the paper, I suggested a simple measure of informativeness *divergence* between a market signal and benchmark risk measures, and showed that – although it cannot be observed directly – it is possible to infer from the function projecting this measure onto a proxy of the extent to which the conditions for market discipline are satisfied which one of the measures that is more informative.

Applying the methodology to a panel of several hundred banks worldwide, with the divergence measure calculated on the basis of three common market-based risk indicators, I find that market-based measures as stand-alone variables are less informative than accounting indicators for most levels of institutional quality.

Stock return volatility is never more informative than accounting measures, but spreads on subordinated debt may be more informative if the conditions for market discipline are well satisfied (for the top 25-30 percent of the observed distribution). This finding raises the question if the failure to find significant associations between subordinated-debt spreads and accounting data in some studies using US data is driven by lower information content in accounting data than in spreads (rather than the other way around, which is the common interpretation). A combination measure incorporating both stock market data and accounting data, finally, is more informative than accounting variables alone for most levels of institutional quality (although the most overall measure of institutional quality used seems to be a relatively weak determinant of the difference in informativeness between the combination risk indicator and the benchmarks). This result is consistent with the results of some previous studies comparing the relative informativeness of different risk indicators, which seem to imply that stock-market data contains information that is complementary to accounting data and other commonly used benchmark risk measures.

REFERENCES

ALLEN, F., BARTILORO, L. and KOWALEWSKI, O. (2006), "The Financial System of EU-25" in K. LIEBSCHER, J. CHRISTL, P. MOOSLECHNER and D. RITZBERGER-GRUNWALD (eds.), *Financial Development, Integration and Stability: Evidence from Central, Eastern, and South-Eastern Europe*, Cheltenham, Edward Elgar.

ANGKINAND, A. and WIHLBORG, C. (2010), "Deposit insurance coverage, ownership, and banks' risk-taking in emerging markets", *Journal of International Money and Finance*, 29, 252-275.

AVERY, R. B., BELTON, T. M., and GOLDBERG, M. A. (1988), "Market Discipline in Regulating Bank Risk: New Evidence form the Capital Markets", *Journal of Money, Credit and Banking*, 20, 597-610.

BARTH, J. R., CAPRIO Jr., G. and LEVINE, R. (2001), "The Regulation and Supervision of Banks around the World: A New Database", *Brookings-Wharton Papers on Financial Services* 2001(1), 183-240.

BARTH, J. R., CAPRIO Jr., G. and LEVINE, R. (2006), *Rethinking Bank Regulation: Till Angels Govern*, Cambridge, Cambridge University Press.

BAUMANN, U. and NIER, E. (2003), "Market discipline and financial stability: some empirical evidence", Bank of England, *Financial Stability Review* (June), 134-141.

BECK, T. and LAEVEN, L. (2006), "Resolution of Failed Banks by Deposit Insurers – Cross-Country Evidence", *Policy Research Working Paper* No. 3920 (May), Washington, DC, The World Bank.

BENINK, H. and WIHLBORG, C. (2002), "The New Basel Capital Accord: Making it Effective with Stronger Market Discipline", *European Financial Management*, 8, 103-115.

BENSTON, G. J. and KAUFMAN, G. G. (1997), "FDICIA after five years", *Journal of Economic Perspectives*, 11, 139-158.

BERGER, A. N. and DAVIES, S. M. (1998), "The Information Content of Bank Examinations", *Journal of Financial Services Research*, 14, 117-144.

BERGER, A. N., DAVIES, S. M. and FLANNERY, M. J. (2000), "Comparing Market and Supervisory Assessments of Bank Performance: Who Knows What When?", *Journal of Money, Credit and Banking*, 32, 641-667.

BIRCHLER, U. W. and HANCOCK, D. (2004), "What Does the Yield on Subordinated Bank Debt Measure?", *FEDS Working Paper*, No. 2004-19 (April).

BLISS, R. R. and FLANNERY, M. J. (2002), "Market discipline in the governance of US bank holding companies: Monitoring vs. influencing", *European Finance Review*, 6, 361-395.

BONGINI, P., LAEVEN, L. and MAJNONI, G. (2002), "How good is the market at assessing bank fragility? A horse race between different indicators", *Journal of Banking and Finance*, 26, 1011-1028.

BOYD, J. H., GRAHAM, S. L. and HEWITT, S. (1993), "Bank holding company mergers with nonbank financial firms: Effects on the risk of failure", *Journal of Banking and Finance*, 17, 43-63.

BOYD, J. H. and DE NICOLÓ, G. (2005), "The Theory of Bank Risk Taking and Competition Revisited", *Journal of Finance*, 60, 1329-1343.

BREWER, E. and MONDSCHEAN, T. H. (1994), "An Empirical Test of the Incentive Effects of Deposit Insurance", *Journal of Money, Credit and Banking*, 26, 146-164.

BRUNE, N., GARRETT, G., GUISINGER, A. and SORENS, J. (2001), "The Political Economy of Capital Account Liberalization", *Working Paper*, Yale University/UCLA.

BUSHMAN, R. M., PIOTROSKI, J. D. and SMITH, A. J. (2004), "What Determines Corporate Transparency?", *Journal of Accounting Research*, 42, 207-252.

CALOMIRIS, C. W. (1999), "Building an incentive-compatible safety net", *Journal of Banking and Finance*, 23, 1499-1519.

COVITZ, D. M., HANCOCK, D. and KWAST, M. L. (2004), "A Reconsideration of the Risk Sensitivity of U.S. Banking Organization Subordinated Debt Spreads: A Sample Selection Approach", Federal Reserve Bank of New York, *Economic Policy Review* (September), 73-92.

CROUZILLE, C., LEPETIT, L. and TARAZI, A. (2004), "Bank stock volatility, news, and asymmetric information in banking: An empirical investigation", *Journal of Multinational Financial Management*, 14, 443-461.

DEMIRGÜÇ-KUNT, A., KARACAOVALI, B. and LAEVEN, L. (2005), "Deposit insurance around the World: A comprehensive database", *Policy Research Working Paper*, No. 3628, Washington, DC, The World Bank.

DEYOUNG, R., FLANNERY, M. J., LANG, W. W. and SORESCU, S. M. (2001), "The information content of bank exam ratings and subordinated debt prices", *Journal of Money, Credit and Banking*, 33, 900-925.

DJANKOV, S., McLIESH, C. and SHLEIFER, A. (2007), "Private Credit in 129 Countries", *Journal of Financial Economics*, 84, 299-329.

DJANKOV, S., LA PORTA, R., LOPEZ-DE-SILANES, F. and SHLEIFER, A. (2006), "The Law and Economics of Self-Dealing", *Journal of Financial Economics*, 88, 430-465.

DURNEV, A., MORCK, R., YEUNG, B. and ZAROWIN, P. (2003), "Does greater firm-specific return variation mean more or less informed stock pricing?", *Journal of Accounting Research*, 41, 797-836.

ELLIS, D. M. and FLANNERY, M. J. (1992), "Does the debt market assess large banks' risk? Time series evidence from money center CDs", *Journal of Monetary Economics*, 30, 481-502.

European Commission (2008), *Risk-based contributions in EU Deposit Guarantee Schemes: current practices*, Final Report on Risk-Based Contributions (June), DG JRC.

EVANOFF, D. and JAGTIANI, J. (2004), *Use of subordinated debt in the supervisory and monitoring process and to enhance market discipline*, mimeo, Federal Reserve Bank of Chicago/Kansas City.

EVANOFF, D. D. and WALL, L. D. (2000), "Subordinated debt and bank capital reform", *Research in Financial Services*, 12, 53-120.

EVANOFF, D. D. and WALL, L. D. (2001), "Sub-debt Yield Spreads as Bank Risk Measures", *Journal of Financial Services Research*, 20, 121-145.

EVANOFF, D. D. and WALL, L. D. (2002), "Measures of the riskiness of banking organizations: Subordinated debt yields, risk-based capital, and examination ratings", *Journal of Banking and Finance*, 26, 989-1009.

FLANNERY, M. J. (2001), "The faces of Market Discipline", *Journal of Financial Services Research*, 20, 107-119.

FLANNERY, M. J. and SORESCU, S. M. (1996), "Evidence of market discipline in subordinated debenture yields: 1983-1991", *Journal of Finance*, 51, 1347-1377.

GORTON, G. and SANTOMERO, A. M. (1990), "Market discipline and bank subordinated debt: Note", *Journal of Money, Credit and Banking*, 22, 119-128.

GOYAL, V. (2005), "Market discipline of bank risk: Evidence from subordinated debt contracts", *Journal of Financial Intermediation*, 14, 318-350.

GROPP, R. and RICHARDS, A. J. (2001), "Rating Agency Actions and the Pricing of Debt and Equity of European Banks: What Can We Infer about Private Sector Monitoring of Bank Soundness?", *Economic Notes* by Banca Monte dei Paschi di Siena 30, 373-398.

GROPP, R., VESALA, J. and VULPES, G. (2006), "Equity and Bond Market Signals as Leading Indicators of Bank Fragility", *Journal of Money, Credit, and Banking*, 38, 399-428.

GUNTHER, J. W., LEVONIAN, M. E. and MOORE, R. R. (2001), "Can the Stock Market Tell Bank Supervisors Anything They Don't Already Know?", Federal Reserve Bank of Dallas *Economic and Financial Review*, No. 2, 2-9.

HALL, J. R., KING, T. B., MEYER, A. P. and VAUGHAN, M. D. (2001), "What Can Bank Supervisors Learn from Equity Markets? A Comparison of the Factors Affecting Market-Based Risk Measures and BOPEC Scores", *Working Paper*, No. 2002-06, Federal Reserve Bank of St. Louis.

HALL, J. R., KING, T. B., MEYER, A. P. and VAUGHAN, M. D. (2004), *Did FDICIA Enhance Market Discipline? A Look at Evidence from the Jumbo-CD Market*, mimeo, Federal Reserve Bank of St Louis (http://ssrn.com/abstract=382101).

HANNAN, T. H. and HANWECK, G. A. (1988), "Bank insolvency risk and the market for large certificates of deposit", *Journal of Money, Credit and Banking*, 20, 203-211.

HECKMAN, J. (1979), "Sample Selection Bias as a Specification Error", *Econometrica*, 47, 153-161.

HONOHAN, P. and LAEVEN, L. (eds.) (2005), *Systemic Financial Crises: Containment and Resolution*, Cambridge, UK, Cambridge University Press.

JAGTIANI, J., KAUFMAN, G. and LEMIEUX, C. (2002), "The effect of credit risk on bank and bank holding company bond yields: Evidence from the post-FDICIA period", *Journal of Financial Research*, 25, 559-575.

JAMES, C. (1988), "The use of loan sales and standby letters of credit by commercial banks", *Journal of Monetary Economics*, 22, 395-422.

JAMES, C. (1990), "Heterogeneous creditors and the market value of bank LDC loan portfolios", *Journal of Monetary Economics*, 25, 325-346.

JORDAN, J. S. (2000), "Depositor discipline at failing banks", *New England Economic Review* (March/April), 15-28.

KEELEY, M. C. (1990), "Deposit insurance, risk, and market power in banking", *American Economic Review*, 80, 1183-1200.

KRAINER, J. and LOPEZ, J. A. (2004), "Incorporating Equity Market Information into Supervisory Monitoring Models", *Journal of Money, Credit and Banking*, 36, 1043-1067.

KRISHNAN, C. N. V., RITCHKEN, P. H. and THOMSON, J. B. (2006), "Monitoring and controlling bank risk: Does risky debt help?", *Journal of Finance*, 61, 1545-1574.

LAEVEN, L. and VALENCIA, F. (2008), "Systemic Banking Crises: A New Database", *Working Paper*, No. WP/08/224 (September), Washington, DC, International Monetary Fund.

LANE, T. D. (1993), "Market discipline", *IMF Staff Papers*, 40, 53-88.

LA PORTA, R., LÓPEZ-DE-SILANES, F., SHLEIFER, A. and VISHNY, R. W. (1997), "Legal Determinants of External Finance", *Journal of Finance*, 52, 1131-1150.

LA PORTA, R., LÓPEZ-DE-SILANES, F., SHLEIFER, A. and VISHNY, R. W. (1998), "Law and Finance", *Journal of Political Economy*, 106, 1113-1155.

LEVONIAN, M. (2001), *Subordinated Debt and the Quality of Market Discipline in Banking*, mimeo (May), Federal Reserve Bank of San Francisco.

LLEWELLYN, D. T. (2005), "Inside the 'Black Box' of Market Discipline", *Economic Affairs*, 25, 41-47.

LOMBARDO, D. and PAGANO, M. (2006), "Legal determinants of the return on equity" in L. OXELHEIM (ed.), *Corporate and Institutional Transparency for Economic Growth in Europe*, Oxford/Amsterdam, Elsevier.

MARTINEZ PERIA, M. S. and SCHMUKLER, S. L. (2001), "Do Depositors Punish Banks for Bad behaviour? Market Discipline, Deposit Insurance, and Banking Crises", *Journal of Finance*, 56, 1029-1051.

MERTON, R. C. (1977), "An analytic derivation of the cost of deposit insurance and loan guarantees", *Journal of Banking and Finance*, 1, 3-11.

MORCK, R., YEUNG, B. and YU, W. (2000), "The information content of stock markets: Why do emerging markets have synchronous stock price movements?", *Journal of Financial Economics*, 58, 215-260.

MORGAN, D. P. and STIROH, K. J. (2001), "Market discipline of banks: The asset test", *Journal of Financial Services Research*, 20, 195-208.

NIVOROZHKIN, E. (2005), "Market discipline of subordinated debt in banking: The case of costly bankruptcy", *European Journal of Operational Research*, 161, 364-376.

PARK, S. (1995), "Market discipline by depositors: Evidence from reduced-form equations", *Quarterly Review of Economics and Finance*, 35, 497-514.

PARK, S. and PERISTIANI, S. (1998), "Market Discipline by Thrift Depositors", *Journal of Money, Credit and Banking*, 30, 347-364.

PENNACHI, G. (2001), "Comments on Morgan and Stiroh", *Journal of Financial Services Research*, 20, 209-211.

PETTWAY, R. H. (1976), "The Effects of Large Bank Failures upon Investors' Risk Cognizance in the Commercial Banking Industry", *Journal of Financial and Quantitative Analysis*, 11, 465-477.

PETTWAY, R. H. (1980), "Potential Insolvency, Market Efficiency, and Bank Regulation of Large Commercial Banks", *Journal of Financial and Quantitative Analysis*, 15, 219-236.

PETTWAY, R. H. and SINKEY, J.F., (1980), "Establishing On-Site Bank Examination Priorities: An Early-Warning System Using Accounting and Market Information", *Journal of Finance*, 35, 137-150.

PISTOR, K., RAISER, M. and GELFER, S. (2000), "Law and Finance in Transition Economies", *Economics of Transition*, 8, 325-368.

POP, A. (2006), "Market discipline in international banking regulation: Keeping the playing field even", *Journal of Financial Stability*, 2, 286-310.

RAJAN, R. G. and ZINGALES, L. (2003), "The great reversals: The politics of financial development in the twentieth century", *Journal of Financial Economics*, 69, 5-50.

SAUNDERS, A. (2001), "Comments on Evanoff and Wall/Hancock and Kwast", *Journal of Financial Services Research*, 20, 189-194.

SIRONI, A. (2001), "An analysis of European banks' SND issues and its implications for the design of a mandatory subordinated debt policy", *Journal of Financial Services Research*, 20, 233-66.

SIRONI, A. (2002), "Strengthening banks' market discipline and leveling the playing field: Are the two compatible?", *Journal of Banking and Finance*, 26, 1065-1091.

SIRONI, A. (2003), "Testing for market discipline in the European banking industry: Evidence from subordinated debt issues", *Journal of Money, Credit and Banking*, 35, 443-472.

YU, F. (2005), "Accounting transparency and the term structure of credit spreads", *Journal of Financial Economics*, 75, 53-84.

APPENDIX A. DERIVATION OF AN EXPRESSION FOR VAR(W)

A bank's 'true' risk is denoted by P (with mean $\bar{P}$ and constant variance). P is unknown, but there are two approximate indicators of P: a market-based indicator, M, and a benchmark indicator, B. From the hypothetical regressions

$$P = \alpha_M + \beta_M M + u \tag{A1}$$

and

$$P = \alpha_B + \beta_B B + v, \tag{A2}$$

define the *informativeness* of M and B, respectively, as $R = 1 - \dfrac{\text{var}(u)}{\text{var}(P)}$, and $R_B^2 = 1 - \dfrac{\text{var}(v)}{\text{var}(P)}$.

Because P is unknown, R_M^2 and R_B^2 are also unknown, and therefore it is not possible to observe directly whether M or B is the more informative indicator of P (i.e., if $R_M^2 < R_B^2$ or $R_M^2 > R_B^2$).

By (A1) and (A2), the simplified 'risk-sensitivity' regression represented by equation (1) in section 3.1 can be rewritten as

$$\frac{P - \alpha_M - u}{\beta_M} = \gamma_0 + \gamma_1 \left(\frac{P - \alpha_B - v}{\beta_B} \right) + w. \tag{A3}$$

Rearranging and simplifying yields

$$w = \delta_1 p + \delta_2 u + \delta_3 v \tag{A4}$$

where the lower-case p denotes deviations from the mean, $\delta_1 = \dfrac{1}{\beta_M} - \dfrac{\gamma_1}{\beta_B}$, $\delta_2 = -\dfrac{1}{\beta_M}$, and $\delta_3 = \dfrac{\gamma_1}{\beta_B}$. Squaring both sides of (A4) and taking expectations generates

$$E(w^2) = \delta_1^2 E(p^2) + \delta_2^2 E(u^2) + \delta_3^2 E(v^2) + 2\delta_1\delta_2 E(pu) + 2\delta_1\delta_3 E(pv) + 2\delta_2\delta_3 E(uv) \tag{A5}$$

or, equivalently,

$$E(w^2) = \delta_1^2 \text{var}(P) + \delta_2^2 \text{var}(u) + \delta_3^2 \text{var}(v) + 2\delta_1\delta_2 \text{cov}(pu) + 2\delta_1\delta_3 \text{cov}(pv) + 2\delta_2\delta_3 \text{cov}(uv) \tag{A6}$$

Since δ_2^2 and δ_3^2 are necessarily positive, $\text{var}(w)$ is a positive function of both $\text{var}(u)$ and $\text{var}(v)$. The covariance between u and v, $\text{cov}(uv)$, will typically affect $\text{var}(w)$ negatively, since $\delta_2\delta_3 = \left(-\dfrac{1}{\beta_M}\right)\dfrac{\gamma_1}{\beta_B} = -\dfrac{\gamma_1}{\beta_M\beta_B} < 0$ provided M and B are positively correlated to each other and to P.

APPENDIX B. TECHNICAL NOTE ON THE ESTIMATION PROCEDURE

B.1. The estimation procedure as an unobserved variables methodology

Let m be a market-based measure of bank risk, b a vector of benchmark risk measures, and z a vector of control variables accounting for known (and observed) differences in variation between m and b that are unrelated to the conditions for market discipline. Market and non-market measures do not contain exactly the same amount of information, so that $E[m|b, z] = \alpha + b\beta + z\gamma + q$, where q captures the difference in informativeness between m and b. Because this difference is unknown, q is unobserved. In this framework, a 'risk-sensitivity' regression can be formulated as:

$$m = \alpha + b\beta + z\gamma + w, \ w \equiv q + \varepsilon \tag{B1}$$

where ε is a random error term. If q is strictly additive and uncorrelated with b, z, a regular OLS regression on the above equation will produce consistent estimates of β and γ. By the inclusion of the intercept term, nothing of the information contained in q is lost, but it does normalize q so that $E[q] = E[\varepsilon] = E[w] = 0$.

With q still unobserved, it can be proxied by $\hat{w}$, since the only other component of $\hat{w}$ is a random error, but because $\hat{w}$ varies around zero, the actual values – positive or negative – do not reveal which measure is more informative, m or b. However, as argued in subsection 3.1, the (absolute) magnitude of the 'divergence' between m and b, measured as $\hat{w}^2$,[18] may vary systematically with the extent to which the conditions for market discipline are satisfied. Thus, the second-step estimations – regressing $\hat{w}^2$ on a proxy of C_{MD} – is an approximate way of testing the relationship between the absolute value of q and the conditions for market discipline.

B.2. Discussion of corrections for panel data

As regards the first-step regressions (equation [2] in section 4.1), the (unbalanced) panel structure of the data introduces some minor issues that need to be addressed. In order not to lose information, the unobserved variable q should be allowed to vary both over time and across firms, but should not be correlated with b, z. Period effects need to be added to account for changes over time that

---

[18]   In order to make the divergence measure comparable for different market-based measures (i.e., comparable for different regressions of the type represented by equation B1, above), the squared *standardized* residuals are used as divergence measure in this paper.

affect all banks equally, but they must be fixed in the cross-section dimension. Adding firm-specific effects, on the other hand, might pick up a significant amount of the information I hope to extract from $\hat{w}$ (insofar as variation in MD conditions is observed at firm-level), so cross-section effects should not be used. Correcting only for a (fixed) time effect will result in serial correlation in $\hat{w}$, which is 'desirable' to the extent that q is expected to be serially correlated and contain firm-specific information which is more or less time-invariant. Since inference on β and γ is not the primary objective, inference-related issues could, in principle, be left aside so long as they are of no direct consequence for producing consistent estimates of β and γ and thus a $\hat{w}$ which is as informative and as good a proxy of q as possible. Nonetheless, since inference at least on β may be of (secondary)[19] interest in itself, standard errors should be corrected for within-cross-section serial correlation.

While for the estimations producing the divergence measures, the necessary panel adjustments are thus more or less given by the underlying assumptions and the objectives of the regressions, for the second-stage regressions (equations [3-5] in section 4.1), they are more of an open issue. Because (fixed) time effects are accounted for in the first-stage regressions, I expect they are of little importance in the residuals obtained from these regressions. Cross-section effects, on the other hand, were considered inappropriate given the small number of observations over time relative to the number of cross-section units (I actually have a single observation for several banks, especially for the divergence measure of sub-debt spreads, for which I have the smallest number of observations). While using cross-section effects would push up the overall explanatory value of the second-stage regressions, interpretation of the coefficients on the principal component(s) of MD conditions would be made difficult with a large portion of the cross-sectional variation being picked up by the cross-section effects. I thus estimate the equations without either period or cross-section effects, but correct standard errors for contemporaneous correlation and cross-section heteroscedasticity.

---

[19] The conclusions one can draw from inference on these regressions are limited, since factors known to influence the relationship between the market-based measure and the benchmark measures – in particular, any number of proxies for the extent to which the conditions for market discipline are satisfied – are *deliberately* left out, in order to lose as little information as possible in the 'divergence' measure.

APPENDIX C. ADDITIONAL DATA TABLES

Table C1. Distribution of banks by country

Country	Number of banks	Average size[a] of included banks in 2005	Number of banks with subordinated debt outstanding in 2005	Average MD conditions of included banks in 2005[b]
Argentina	4	4,853	2	-3.09
Australia	9	55,698	9	2.84
Austria	4	18,625	4	-0.68
Brazil	14	13,558	6	-3.79
Canada	9	90,587	8	4.41
Chile	5	14,229	3	-1.14
Colombia	11	2,244	1	-3.48
Czech Republic	1	20,942	0	-2.60
Denmark	40	847	25	2.11
Egypt	20	978	1	-2.41
Finland	2	8,201	2	2.06
France	11	22,495	5	1.08
Germany	16	11,632	8	-0.10
Greece	10	13,638	5	-0.63
Hong Kong	7	15,165	3	5.12
Hungary	2	5,265	2	-2.64
India	37	13,051	10	-2.73
Indonesia	22	4,154	9	-3.28
Ireland	5	127,953	5	2.30
Israel	8	16,406	5	0.06
Italy	19	28,383	13	-0.78
Japan	87	19,133	54	0.91
Kenya	7	575	0	-4.79
South Korea	8	33,349	3	-1.31
Lithuania	4	955	3	-1.70
Malaysia	3	28,277	3	0.53
Malta	4	1,425	1	-0.21
Morocco	5	6,241	1	-2.79
Netherlands	1	1,039,000	1	4.59
Pakistan	20	1,345	8	-2.94
Peru	9	948	3	-2.19
Philippines	15	1,626	8	-2.11
Poland	12	6,548	2	-2.96
Portugal	3	73,289	3	0.28
Romania	3	1,472	1	-3.43
Singapore	2	71,652	2	3.33
South Africa	2	5,477[c]	1	-1.66[d]
Spain	14	25,982	9	1.78
Sri Lanka	7	658	4	n.a.
Sweden	2	217,181	2	2.92
Switzerland	6	6,780	3	3.90
Taiwan	15	11,636	5	-0.46

Country	Number of banks	Average size[a] of included banks in 2005	Number of banks with subordinated debt outstanding in 2005	Average MD conditions of included banks in 2005[b]
Thailand	13	7,679	11	-1.48
Turkey	12	8,183	3	-2.78
United Kingdom	3	18,409	2	4.48
United States	15	3,511	6	3.34
Venezuela	14	1,027	0	-4.78

n.a.: Not available.
Notes: a) Total assets in millions of USD. b) Index of the conditions for market discipline given by the first principal component of variables listed in Table A3, Panel B. A higher value indicates better conditions for market discipline. Total sample observations on the index run between -6.69 and 5.78 and have zero mean. c) Refers to average size in 2004 (no observations for 2005). d) Refers to average MD conditions in 2002 (no observations for 2003-2005).

Table C2. Distribution of observations on market-based risk measures over time

Year	Risk measure, number of obs's		
	Sub-debt spreads	Stock return volatility	Market Z-score
1994	10	299	0
1995	10	333	1
1996	14	344	1
1997	23	375	23
1998	34	395	227
1999	38	415	273
2000	51	431	301
2001	61	448	321
2002	70	461	341
2003	89	475	357
2004	103	489	433
2005	134	499	410

Table C3, Panel A. Risk measures (market- and accounting-based) and control variables

Variable	Description	Source
Market-based risk measures		
Subordinated debt spreads	Spread over equal-maturity riskfree rate of yields on the bank's subordinated bonds or notes, in basis points	Datastream, Reuters
Stock return volatility	Standard deviation of daily equity returns (calculated for each year)	Datastream
Z-score	(Average return on equity – equity capital over total assets) divided by standard deviation of equity returns	Datastream, BankScope
Accounting-based risk measures		
Leverage	One minus the equity share of total assets	BankScope
Non-performing loans	Non-performing loans divided by equity capital	As above
Liquid assets	Liquid assets divided by total assets	As above
Return on assets (ROA)	Net earnings divided by total assets	As above
Bank-level control variables		
Deposits	Deposits divided by total assets	As above
Net interest margin	Interest income over interest expenditure	As above
Cost/income ratio	Total costs divided by total income	As above
Country-level control variables		
Real interest rate	Real interest rate	World Development Indicators
Inflation	Annual change in consumer prices	As above
Growth	Real GDP growth	As above
Systemic financial crisis	Dummy variable equal to one if the country was undergoing a systemic financial crisis, zero otherwise	Honohan and Laeven (2005); Laeven and Valencia (2008)

Table C3, Panel B. Proxies of conditions for market discipline

		Bank-level variables	Source	Country-level variables	Source
Monitoring	Open capital markets	Turnover rate[a]	Datastream	Bank deposits (or M2)/GDP	IMF's IFS + World Bank's WDI
				Private-sector credit/GDP	As above
				Equity issues/Gross Fixed Capital Formation[g]	Datastream, Eurostat + IFS or WDI
				Equity market capitalization/GDP	As above
				Number of publicly traded firms/mn. population	Datastream + WDI
				Corporate bond market capitalization/GDP	Bank for International Settlements/ IMF's IFS
				Foreign-investment openness[h]	Brune et al. (2001)
	Good information			Corporate transparency/private monitoring index[i]	Bushman et al. (2004), Barth et al. (2001, 2006)
	No bailout	Share of formally insured debt[b]	BankScope, Demirgüç-Kunt et al. (2005)		
		No-bailout credibility[c]	Fitch/BankScope + IMF's IFS		
		Government ownership dummy[d]	Reuters		
Influence	Responsiveness to market signals	Institutional ownership[e]	Reuters	Shareholder rights index[j]	La Porta et al., 1997, 1998; Pistor et al., 2000; Djankov et al., 2007, 2008; and Allen et al., 2006
		Insider ownership[e]	Reuters	Creditor rights index[j]	As above
		Excess capital[f]	BankScope, Barth et al. (2001, 2006)	Index of rule of law	International Country Risk Guide

Notes:
a) Average daily turnover divided by market value of equity.
b) Country-wide deposit insurance coverage in percent multiplied by each bank's ratio of deposits to total debt (equals zero for banks from countries with no explicit deposit insurance).
c) The Fitch support index of probability of bailout, wherever available, otherwise one minus the bank's share of total deposits (alt. M2) in its country of residence.
d) Dummy variable equal to one if the largest insider/stakeholder is the government.
e) Equity held by institutional investors and insiders, respectively, divided by all equity.
f) The equity share of total assets minus the applicable regulatory Tier-1 capital requirement, defined as 50% of the total capital requirement.
g) Net equity issues are approximated as the year-on-year change in a country's stock market capitalization, corrected for the change in stock prices as measured by Datastream's overall market price index for each country; the variable used is an average of observations for 1995-2005.
h) Index of capital-account openness based on nine categories of capital-account transactions as reported in IMF's Annual Report on Exchange Arrangements and Exchange Restrictions.
i) Equals the score on CIFAR's (Center for Financial Analysis and Research) overall index of financial-reporting transparency, wherever available, otherwise Barth et al. (2001, 2006) Private Monitoring index, recalculated to the CIFAR index scale.
j) Antidirector rights and creditor rights index, respectively; originally from La Porta et al. (1997, 1998); additional sources are for countries included in this paper's country sample but not in La Porta et al. (1998) are Allen et al., (2006), Djankov et al. (2007, 2008), and Pistor et al. (2000).

Table C4. Pairwise correlations, bank-level benchmark risk measures and control variables

	Leverage	Non-performing loans	Liquidity	ROA	Deposit share	Net interest margin
Non-performing loans	0.375					
Liquidity	-0.116	-0.089				
ROA	-0.423	-0.463	0.185			
Deposit share	0.512	0.216	-0.124	-0.236		
Net interest margin	-0.361	-0.219	0.149	0.385	-0.189	
Cost/income ratio	0.049	0.142	0.035	-0.412	0.004	-0.024

Table C5. Pairwise correlations, conditions for market discipline

Panel A. Bank-level variables

	Turnover rate	Share of formally insured debt	No-bailout credibility	Institutional ownership	Inside ownership
Share of formally insured debt	-0.024				
No-bailout credibility	-0.049	-0.171			
Institutional ownership	0.140	-0.045	-0.273		
Inside ownership	-0.060	-0.002	-0.032	-0.344	
Excess capital	0.088	-0.118	0.278	-0.003	0.067

Table C5. Pairwise correlations, conditions for market discipline (continued)

Panel B. Country-level variables

	Bank deposits/ GDP	Private sector credit/GDP	Equity issues/ investment	Equity market cap./ GDP	Listed firms/ mn. population	Corporate bond market cap./GDP	Foreign-investment openness	Corporate transparency / private monitoring	Shareholder rights	Creditor rights
Private sector credit/GDP	0.671									
Equity issues/investment	0.434	0.319								
Equity market cap./GDP	0.619	0.647	0.635							
Listed firms/mn. Population	0.529	0.320	0.521	0.535						
Corporate bond market cap./GDP	0.171	0.521	0.076	0.380	0.190					
Foreign-investment openness	0.349	0.431	0.284	0.510	0.380	0.677				
Corporate transparency/private monitoring	0.428	0.503	0.285	0.524	0.479	0.464	0.452			
Shareholder rights	0.233	0.226	0.219	0.238	0.299	-0.158	-0.272	0.290		
Creditor rights	-0.013	-0.180	-0.400	-0.243	-0.011	-0.088	-0.126	-0.104	-0.001	
Rule of law	0.481	0.515	0.190	0.496	0.479	0.572	0.539	0.568	0.145	0.010

Table C6. Estimation results of the sub-debt sample selection model

The table shows coefficient estimates from a pooled probit regression of the selection indicator (a dummy variable indicating if the bank had sub-debt outstanding during the observation year) on bank- and country-level regressors[a]. T-statistics in parentheses are based on regular probit standard errors (and should therefore be interpreted with caution, given the panel structure of the dataset). Observation-specific estimates of the inverse Mills ratio from this model were used as an additional explanatory variable in Table 5's model (2) to account for possible sample-selection bias.

	Dependent variable: Sub-debt dummy
Leverage	6.47 (5.89)***
Non-performing loans	-0.12 (-1.98)**
Liquid assets	-0.43 (-1.73)*
Return on assets (ROA)	0.064 (0.020)
Real interest rate	0.90 (1.82)*
Inflation	-0.49 (-0.81)
Growth	0.22 (0.17)
(Sub-debt dummy)$_{t-1}$	2.76 (32.7)***
Undercapitalization dummy	0.58 (4.15)***
Intercept	-6.93 (-6.79)***
McFadden pseudo-R^2	0.59
Regression likelihood ratio	2030***
No. of observations (of which dep. var. = 1)	2496 (1228)
No. of banks	437

*/**/*** denotes significance at 10/5/1 percent confidence level.

Note: a) To my knowledge, Covitz et al. (2004) were first to use the Heckman (1979) two-step approach to correct for sample-selection bias in the context of risk-sensitivity tests on sub-debt spreads. They estimate a model where the bank's decision to issue sub-debt is a function of the bank's own risk level, macroeconomic and market conditions, firm-specific advantages, and the regulatory pressure to issue. I based the above model on that general structure, and variables are grouped accordingly in the table. Proxies for bank risk and macroeconomic variables need no explanation or motivation. Firm-specific advantages are summarized by the lagged sub-debt dummy (used also by Covitz et al., 2004) since it can reasonably be assumed that this variable is strongly serially correlated within cross-section units; Covitz et al. (2004) use examination ratings to measure regulatory pressure to issue capital (which could be at least in part sub-debt); such ratings are not available for cross-country samples, and I instead use the undercapitalization dummy to proxy for the pressure to issue.

APPENDIX D.

Table D1. Summary of risk indicators used in previous studies on market discipline in banking

Market-based risk indicators	
Equity-based	
Equity return volatility (various definitions)	Brewer and Mondschean (1994); Hall *et al.* (2001); James (1988, 1990)
Abnormal equity returns (market model)[a]	Berger and Davies (1998); Berger *et al.* (2000); Birchler and Hancock (2004); Bliss and Flannery (2002); Gropp and Richards (2001); Krainer and Lopez (2004); Pettway (1976, 1980); Pettway and Sinkey (1980)
Beta (CAPM or market model)	Gunther *et al.* (2001); Hall *et al.* (2001)
Other, equity-based	Bliss and Flannery (2002); Ellis and Flannery (1992); Hall *et al.* (2001); Krainer and Lopez (2004)
Debt-based	
Primary-market spreads on subordinated notes and bonds	Evanoff and Jagtiani (2004); Goyal (2005); Morgan and Stiroh (2001); Sironi (2002, 2003)
Secondary-market spreads on subordinated notes and bonds	Avery *et al.* (1988); Birchler and Hancock (2004); Covitz *et al.* (2004); DeYoung *et al.* (2001); Evanoff and Jagtiani (2004); Evanoff and Wall (2001, 2002); Flannery and Sorescu (1996); Gorton and Santomero (1990); Gropp *et al.* (2006); Jagtiani *et al.* (2002); Krishnan *et al.* (2006); Pop (2006)
Interest rate spreads on large certificates of deposit (CDs)	Brewer and Mondschean (1994); Ellis and Flannery (1992); Hall *et al.* (2004); Hannan and Hanweck (1988); James (1988, 1990); Jordan (2000); Keeley (1990)
Other, debt-based[b]	Birchler and Hancock (2004); Bliss and Flannery (2002); Gropp and Richards (2001); Martinez Peria and Schmukler (2001); Park (1995); Park and Perestiani (1998); Pop (2006)
Accounting-based risk indicators	
Capital-structure-based	
Leverage, or capital ratio (various definitions, e.g. equity/total assets, liabilities/market or book value of equity, etc.)	Avery *et al.* (1988); Berger *et al.* (2000); Birchler and Hancock (2004); Bliss and Flannery (2002); Brewer and Mondschean (1994); Covitz *et al.* (2004); DeYoung *et al.* (2001); Evanoff and Jagtiani (2004); Evanoff and Wall (2001, 2002); Flannery and Sorescu (1996); Goyal (2005); Gropp *et al.* (2006); Gunther *et al.* (2001); Hall *et al.* (2001, 2004); Hannan and Hanweck (1988); Jagtiani *et al.* (2002); James (1988); Keeley (1990); Krainer and Lopez (2004); Krishnan *et al.* (2006); Martinez Peria and Schmukler (2001); Morgan and Stiroh (2001); Park and Perestiani (1998); Park (1995); Sironi (2003)
Debt or deposit structure[c]	Bliss and Flannery (2002); Evanoff and Jagtiani (2004); Gunther *et al.* (2001); Hall *et al.* (2004); Jagtiani *et al.* (2002); Park (1995)
Loan- or asset-structure-based	
Non-performing loans or similar (non-accruing loans, loans past due, etc)/total assets	Avery *et al.* (1988); Berger and Davies (1998); Berger *et al.* (2000); Birchler and Hancock (2004); Bliss and Flannery (2002); Covitz *et al.* (2004); DeYoung *et al.* (2001); Evanoff and Jagtiani (2004); Flannery and Sorescu (1996); Gorton and Santomero (1990); Gropp *et al.* (2006); Gunther *et al.* (2001); Hall *et al.* (2001, 2004); Jagtiani *et al.* (2002); Krainer and Lopez (2004); Krishnan *et al.* (2006); Martinez Peria and Schmukler (2001); Morgan and Stiroh (2001); Park and Perestiani (1998); Park (1995)
Loan-loss provisions or loan-loss reserves/total loans or total assets	Avery *et al.* (1988); Baumann and Nier (2003); Berger and Davies (1998); Bliss and Flannery (2002); Bongini *et al.* (2002); Gunther *et al.* (2001); James (1988); Krainer and Lopez (2004); Krishnan *et al.* (2006); Sironi (2003)

Other, loan structure[d]	Avery *et al.* (1988); Bliss and Flannery (2002); Brewer and Mondschean (1994); Hall *et al.* (2004); James (1990); Krishnan *et al.* (2006); Martin (1977); Martinez Peria and Schmukler (2001); Morgan and Stiroh (2001); Park and Peristiani (1998)
Non-loan asset structure[e]	Avery *et al.* (1988); Birchler and Hancock (2004); Bliss and Flannery (2002); Bongini *et al.* (2002); Brewer and Mondschean (1994); Covitz *et al.* (2004); DeYoung *et al.* (2001); Evanoff and Jagtiani (2004); Flannery and Sorescu (1996); Gunther *et al.* (2001); Hall *et al.* (2001, 2004); Krainer and Lopez (2004); Martin (1977); Martinez Peria and Schmukler (2001); Morgan and Stiroh (2001); Park and Peristiani (1998); Park (1995); Saunders *et al.* (1990); Sironi (2003)
Profitability-based	
Return on assets[f]	Avery *et al.* (1988); Berger *et al.* (2000); Bliss and Flannery (2002); Bongini *et al.* (2002); DeYoung *et al.* (2001); Evanoff and Jagtiani (2004); Flannery and Sorescu (1996); Gropp *et al.* (2006); Gunther *et al.* (2001); Hall *et al.* (2001, 2004); Jagtiani *et al.* (2002); Krainer and Lopez (2004); Krishnan *et al.* (2006); Martinez Peria and Schmukler (2001); Morgan and Stiroh (2001); Park and Peristiani (1998); Park (1995); Sironi (2003)
Earnings volatility	Avery *et al.* (1988)
Other, accounting-based	Birchler and Hancock (2004); Bongini *et al.* (2002); Covitz *et al.* (2004); DeYoung *et al.* (2001); Flannery and Sorescu (1996); Gorton and Santomero (1990); Gropp *et al.* (2006); Hall *et al.* (2001); James (1988); Morgan and Stiroh (2001)
Combination measures[g]	Bongini *et al.* (2002); Gorton and Santomero (1990); Gropp *et al.* (2006); Gunther *et al.* (2001); Hannan and Hanweck (1988); Krainer and Lopez (2004)
Ratings	
Rating agencies' bond issue ratings	Berger *et al.* (2000); DeYoung *et al.* (2001); Flannery and Sorescu (1996); Goyal (2005); Gropp and Richards (2001); Jagtiani *et al.* (2002); Krishnan *et al.* (2006); Morgan and Stiroh (2001); Sironi (2002, 2003)
Rating agencies' issuer (bank) ratings	Avery *et al.* (1988); Bongini *et al.* (2002); Evanoff and Jagtiani (2004); Gropp *et al.* (2006); Pop (2006); Sironi (2002, 2003)
Examination/supervisory ratings (CAMEL/BOPEC)[h]	Berger and Davies (1998); Berger *et al.* (2000); DeYoung *et al.* (2001); Evanoff and Jagtiani (2004); Evanoff and Wall (2001, 2002); Gunther *et al.* (2001); Hall *et al.* (2001); Jagtiani *et al.* (2002); Krainer and Lopez (2004); Krishnan *et al.* (2006)

Notes:
a) Used to detect market reactions to events or information that may signal changes in bank risk, rather than as an explicit risk indicator.
b) Regular deposit interest rates, spreads on senior bonds, etc.
c) Jumbo or brokered CDs/total assets, insured deposits/total assets, etc.
d) Loan assets/total assets, commercial and industrial loans/total assets, residential real estate loans/total assets, renegotiated loans/total assets, etc.
e) Liquid assets/total assets, fixed or tangible assets/total assets, trading assets or investment securities/total assets, repossessed assets/total assets, etc.
f) Used mainly as a control variable.
g) These indicators use both market prices and accounting data; the category includes option-pricing-based measures (implied volatility, implicit deposit insurance premium, etc.) and the Z-score used in this paper.
h) These are composite ratings assigned by the US federal supervisory agencies following on-site examinations of banking firms (CAMEL) or BHCs (BOPEC). They are thus only applicable to US datasets.

SUERF – Société Universitaire Européenne de Recherches Financières

SUERF is incorporated in France as a non-profit-making Association. It was founded in 1963 as a European-wide forum with the aim of bringing together professionals from both the practitioner and academic sides of finance who have an interest in the working of financial markets, institutions and systems, and the conduct of monetary and regulatory policy. SUERF is a network association of central bankers, bankers and other practitioners in the financial sector, and academics with the purpose of analysing and understanding European financial markets, institutions and systems, and the conduct of regulation and monetary policy. It organises regular Colloquia, lectures and seminars and each year publishes several analytical studies in the form of *SUERF Studies*.

SUERF has its full-time permanent Executive Office and Secretariat located at the Austrian National Bank in Vienna. It is financed by annual corporate, personal and academic institution membership fees. Corporate membership currently includes major European financial institutions and Central Banks. SUERF is strongly supported by Central Banks in Europe and its membership comprises most of Europe's Central Banks (including the Bank for International Settlements and the European Central Bank), banks, other financial institutions and academics.

SUERF Studies

1997-2010

For details of SUERF Studies published prior to 2010 (Nos. 1 to 22 and 2003/1-2009/5) please consult the SUERF website at www.suerf.org.

2010

2010/1   *Crisis Management at cross-roads – Challenges facing cross-border financial institutions at the EU level*, edited by Rym Ayadi, Morten Balling and Frank Lierman, Vienna 2010, ISBN 978-3-902109-51-4

2010/2   *The Quest for stability: the macro view*, edited by Morten Balling, Jan Marc Berk and Marc-Olivier Strauss-Kahn, Vienna 2010, 978-3-902109-52-1

2010/3   *The Quest for stability: the view of financial institutions*, edited by Morten Balling, Jan Marc Berk and Marc-Olivier Strauss-Kahn, Vienna 2010, 978-3-902109-53-8

2010/4   *The Quest for stability: The financial stability view*, edited by Morten Balling, Jan Marc Berk and Marc-Olivier Strauss-Kahn, Vienna 2010, 978-3-902109-54-5

2010/5   *Contagion and Spillovers: New Insights from the Crisis*, edited by Peter Backé, Ernest Gnan and Philipp Hartmann, Vienna, 978-3-902109-55-2

2011

2011/1   *The Future of Banking in CESEE after the Financial Crisis*, edited by Attilla Csajbók and Ernest Gnan, Vienna 2011, ISBN 978-3-902109-56-9

2011/2   *Regulation and Banking after the Crisis*, edited by Frank Browne, David T. Llewellyn and Philip Molyneux, Vienna 2011, ISBN 978-3-902109-57-6

2011/3   *Monetary Policy after the Crisis*, edited by Ernest Gnan, Ryszard Kokoszczynski, Tomasz Łyziak and Robert McCauley, Vienna 2011, ISBN 978-3-902109-58-3